Fierce and Tender Men

Until one is committed there is hesitancy, the chance to draw back, always ineffectiveness. Concerning all acts of initiative (and creation), there is one elementary truth the ignorance of which kills countless ideas and splendid plans: that the moment one definitely commits oneself, then providence moves too.

All sorts of things occur to help one that would never otherwise have occurred. A whole stream of events issues from the decision, raising in one's favour all manner of unforseen incidents and meetings and material assistance, which no man could have dreamed could come his way.

Whatever you can do or dream you can, begin it. Boldness has genius, power and magic in it. Begin it now.

· Goethe ·

FIERCE and TENDER MEN

Sociological Aspects of the Men's Movement

Clinton J. Jesser

PRAEGER

**Westport, Connecticut
London**

Library of Congress Cataloging-in-Publication Data

Jesser, Clinton J.
    Fierce and tender men : sociological aspects of the men's movement /
Clinton J. Jesser.
        p. cm.
    Includes bibliographical references and index.
    ISBN 0–275–95345–9 (alk. paper).—ISBN 0–275–95521–4 (pbk. :
alk. paper)
        1. Men—Social conditions. 2. Men—Psychology. 3. Men's
    movement. 4. Masculinity (Psychology). 5. Sex role. I. Title.
    HQ1090.J47   1996
    305.32—dc 20   95–45420

British Library Cataloguing in Publication Data is available.

Library of Congress Catalog Card Number: 95–45420
ISBN: 0–275–95345–9
        0–275–95521–4 (pbk.)

First published in 1996

Praeger Publishers, 88 Post Road West, Westport, CT 06881
An imprint of Greenwood Publishing Group, Inc.

Printed in the United States of America

∞™

The paper used in this book complies with the
Permanent Paper Standard issued by the National
Information Standards Organization (Z39.48–1984).

10 9 8 7 6 5 4 3 2 1

To all men because we are unfinished

Contents

Preface

"Gradually, without seeing it clearly for quite a while, I came to realize that something is very wrong with the way American women are trying to live their lives today," wrote Betty Friedan in 1963.[1] Soon after, a vast amount of activity followed or was already developing: a flood of treatises/textbooks on women, by and for women, campaigns for employment and legal developments, and the rise of a host of new women's organizations. A full-fledged women's movement emerged.

The time was right. These authors and advocates opened our eyes. Most found inequality and discrimination the guiding concepts and sought in their analyses to uncover the mechanisms by which these are perpetuated both at the level of socialization (upbringing) and at the level of large social institutions and organizations in our society. Little was said about men in the many books I read, maybe because the women authors did not want to speak for them, perhaps because space did not permit, or because they assumed everyone already knew about male identity. What was sometimes said or implied was that there was a (destructive) male "sex role" (big, violent, competitive) or that a few men were "profeminist."

Many men today sense an uneasiness similar to that detected by Friedan for women in 1963. I see it in the men who enroll in the courses I teach on gender in the university as well as among men elsewhere. This book is primarily for them as well as all readers (men *and* women) who want another point of view on gender and men's lives in particular. This book is both a scholarly analysis and a personal-experience account of the men's movement with respect to some issues and promises it raises and makes.

But is there a men's movement? That depends on our definition. A social movement is generally defined as an organized grouping of people that emerges to right some wrong. A movement grows by awakening people and changing institutional policies and arrangements in the society on the basis of a strong moral sentiment, which shows the wrong to be intolerable. Examples are: the National Farmers Organization (NFO), the American Indian Movement (AIM), the civil-rights movement, and the antipornography movement.

I see some resemblance to the general stages of germinating social movements in the stirrings of men in the last decade. First, there is some, usually murky, sense of dissatisfaction in one's life—rumblings that something is "out of kilter"; there is a period of discussion, at first faltering, but finally some clearer raising of consciousness among the distressed that identifies the struggle, the anomalies, the deficits, or the *ennui*. In present men's work, the notion of a "wound," arising from such sources as isolation, father absence, unspoken shame, lack of initiation, and mentoring, and the unjustified scapegoating of men, serve as examples. Some of the discussion in this book addresses this phase of social movements. Finally, there is usually another stage, mobilization, in which plans of action for change or healing are implemented. This might involve personal—for example emotional—work as well as organized efforts to change the policies, stereotypes, and customs of our society. There is also, as I shall show momentarily, resistance (sometimes *nasty* resistance) to social movements and suspicions about men going off by themselves for a weekend of healing and encounter. We might quibble over the word "movement," but there is a rise of interest in men's issues, and, as Warren Farrell, author of the *Myth of Male Power*, has noted, a need to "balance out" the sexism on both sides and develop what he calls a healthy and compassionate "gender transition" for men too.[2]

In the language of social movements, it appears that women's and men's concerns don't closely parallel each other. The benchmarks for women historically were the rewards and rights of men, especially those in their same social class or above them, against an historical background of oppression; for men, the concern is often more about What's missing? like a gap in identity, human passion, and vision. Why am I working harder but getting less out of life and not appreciated? Why aren't some family social services available to us? Why are more of us in prison, committing suicide and living shorter lives than women? Is it just testosterone poisoning? Maybe we need a *human* movement for all.

I've fashioned and arranged the first part of this book along the lines of a journey. That rubric seemed to come naturally as I looked at men's lives. By journey, I mean a process of taking conscious account of what's taking place throughout our lives—the continuities and discontinuities, the struggle for meaning, purpose, and dignity. There is a sense of both order and change that can encourage us to be aware of what is going on both in the larger society and in our own personal lives. The journey begins at birth and ends at death. Historically, what is very interesting here, is that in the last forty years we have discovered lots of methods to both clarify and enrich our trip. This variety ranges from personal diary keeping to support groups, and they are discussed in this book. Crises, as I shall show, are also important to the journey of many of us, especially in the ways that we interpret what they mean and how we handle their challenges.

The last part of the book speaks more for men on the court (rather than in the safer seats on the sidelines), calling for a more active intervention in promoting our own well-being, to building a supportive culture, and finding possibilities of our healing, mission, and enjoyment. Kierkegaard said that "Life can only be understood backwards, but it must be lived forwards." Here we will do *both*—look backward and forward. In a way, I see Robert Bly (and others) urging men onto the courts when interviewed in "What Do Men Really Want?"[3] His story-telling and commitment will be appreciated by thousands of men for years to come. Finally, I shall suggest the possibility of men's groups—men feeding each other nourishing sustenance.

My intention is to open a new conversation that surveys the intersection of social structure (the larger society) and social character (biography)—personal life in society—but with emphasis on break-throughs in passages, commitments, and stance in life. In other words, I utilize an analytical and an action-research point of view (a praxis if you like) in regard to these questions: what are men's lives like, what do men need to know, what can they do to make a difference in their lives? In the last chapters of this book, I explore connections in the areas of gender, biography, and recovery/support groups in the men's movement as well as within twelve-step work generally. Indeed it was only while I was observing and participating in both men's work and Al-Anon that I saw the rich intersections of the two and their crucial relationship to gender concerns.

A word about the phrase "creating and taking a stand" is in order. I use the word "stand," especially in the last part of this book, not as a stubborn position from which to do battle, make others wrong, or resist the oppressors who have victimized us, but rather as a process by which a man creates something in his voice (I call it a "project" in Chapter 9) and makes it present in his action (as results), often with the support-participation of other people. The stand can pertain either to himself or to his mission. It is usually something bigger than his past. It is not a pipe dream, which has little chance of fulfillment, but the leverage implied in Archimedes' saying, "Give me a place to stand [near its curvature] and I will move the earth." A stand is born of vision and allows us to see that, if it is to be fulfilled, committed action (on the court of life) must follow. More precisely, a stand guides the way to action.

It is absolutely essential to emphasize that this book is *not* intended as a defense of men who 1) do not share housework and childcare tasks, 2) support homophobia or discriminate against people whose orientation is homosexual, 3) embrace blind militarism or senseless violence, or 4) resist equality for women.

I want to briefly mention what I take as the precarious position of a men's studies discussion at the present time, especially one which commiserates with men's struggles. Recently, I attended a large regional sociology convention as I have done for many years. One session on the program, "Men and Masculinity," caught my attention. Four white men (all academicians) had prepared papers on the general topic, which they read one after the other. At least two of these were highly sarcastic intellectual attacks on "the" men's movement (if it doesn't include *all* men and especially men of color, apologize for all the sins of patriarchy over the last ten thousand years, and fix all the worlds inequities and problems, we should forget it), men's work (we're just whining babies who already hold all the power and privilege), and men's groups, and especially ritual in groups (we're just pretentious). Of course Robert Bly, an activist in the men's movement, was attacked too, but it wasn't clear if the attacker had actually read Bly's *Iron John*[4], which he was attacking. At the end of the session, finally, a person in the audience asked the telling question: "Are any of you men actually in an ongoing men's group?" Silence. Not one was. What can men in the movement do about this? Correct the false generalizations when they appear, tell their own story, and invite them into a men's group.

In Chapter 3, I lay out my own autobiography with some humility and trepidation. I want to supplement that here. I have been teaching and researching the topic of sex and gender for much of my thirty-two years in academia as a professor of sociology. I also was involved in setting up the first women's shelter in my community and in creating the first women's studies program at my university. I also cotaught one of the foundation courses in that program. Though I am grateful for the growth I attained there and I still respect these programs, it was here that I first realized that men were being left out and that I felt very uncomfortable with that. Even women in the program came to me informally to say they were getting only "half-truths."

The turning point came only six years ago when I became involved with a variety of programs, encounters, gatherings, and workshops I call men's work. In doing that, however, I saw myself becoming somewhat marginal to the university where I worked; Was Professor Jesser losing his objectivity? Aren't men privileged already, and brutal too? I knew "they" misunderstood, but I didn't always have time for the dialogue I felt was needed. If this book accomplishes a bridge of understanding between academic suspicion and men's lives seen in a more compassionate manner, I will be happy. I'm including an Evaluation section after most of the chapters for that purpose.

It was, however, with my students that a pleasant surprise awaited me in the "Sex and Gender" course. The textbooks had been, over the years, mainly about women's issues. More recently as I brought in a few books and videos on men's lives and gatherings and honestly shared regarding my own journey and metamorphosis as a man, it was as though I was speaking into a hunger eager to hear, into a void waiting to be filled. I went out of my way to show how men's and women's studies (and movements) need not pursue different ultimate goals. The written anonymous evaluations at the end of the semester indicated that 98 percent of the students found this material highly informative.

It's appropriate to say a word about the content and placement of the chapters in this book. There are many topics critical to men's lives. I've chosen several: The society in which they live (Chapter 2), their own development and change through time (Chapter 3), some aspects of their growing up, especially the role of parents (Chapter 4), sex, fatherhood, and work (Chapters 5, 6, and 7), and, finally, men's isolation and the role of men's groups in ending that (Chapters 8 and 9). The progression of the chapters seemed logical to me, but there is a jump between the second and the third chapters—from considerations regarding the larger milieu of our society (Chapter 2) and our personal lives as we experience them (Chapter 3). Taking action for most men will probably involve work on both fronts, so I felt I needed to discuss them both. The last two chapters lead to some possibilities of action, even some suggestions on how to do it. I realize that this is uncustomary in academic books, but since some of the discussion emanates from a social-movement point of view, these chapters were needed.

This book was a long time coming. In a way, I say that I've been in encounter with gender roles, consciously or unconsciously, since I was eight years old, when I had my first serious girlfriend (see my autobiography, Chapter 3). The feminist movement of the 1960s and 1970s, especially as that was translated to me by (now) my ex-wife and by many other educated women in our social and professional circles, was a big factor. I carried much of this influence, and my reaction to it, into my research and into my teaching, especially into the Gender and Sex in Society class I've mentioned earlier. The biggest factor, however, has been my participation in some confrontational and healing men's work, which continues to leave me in touch with men as friends and mentors that seemed impossible for me ten years ago.

Specifically, the book was born one night four years ago when Lynda (a woman whose company I enjoy) and I were driving back to DeKalb from a trip, and she began to ask me about my family background and the turning points of my life over a period of my sixty years. I could see the book taking shape at that point and I knew I had to put *myself* into it in terms of my own biography, experiences, and observations (Chapter 3). I've enjoyed that. Many of the insights came to me while jogging, lying in the bathtub soaking in warm-water bubbles, or in bed when I was trying to get to sleep at night. I've also enjoyed stepping out of sociology to some extent and seeing what writers/researchers in other fields have been doing.

Some (many) acknowledgments are in order:

1. Thanks to my many students over the years, especially in my Sex and Gender classes, for their feedback, which included reading earlier drafts of Chapters 2, 8, and 9.

2. Thanks to my New Warrior brothers—they're on the cutting edge of a huge challenge.

3. Thanks to Rich Tosi, Bill Kauth, Randall Borkus, and David Lindgren for showing me their fierceness and tenderness.

4. Warren Farrell gave me encouragement when I needed it and so did Christine Peters, Aaron Kipnis, Laurel Richardson, James Doyle, Earl Babbie, and Ed Barton.

5. Steve Smith, Jim Thomas, Chris Harding, and Michael Gurian went beyond the call of duty in giving me highly useful critique of the manuscript. Suzanne Merkel gave me a good feminist critique of Chapter 5. Thanks to Marilyn, my ex-spouse, who read Chapter 3.

6. Robert Bly has been a deep inspiration to me, and I also thank him for reading Chapter 8.

7. Thanks go to Joe Gastiger, Ruth Rhoads, and Michael Malan for reading/editing and to Sue Barkman who whipped the text out of her word processor in record time. Thanks also to Liz Murphy, my editor at Praeger. She brought a spirit of availability, expertise, and commitment that I cherish.

8. Thanks to my son, Nathan, who demands a lot of himself.

9. Finally, I want to thank my daughter, Lisa. In her place of work as a nurse practitioner, one day, one of her colleagues (all women) mentioned the men's movement, and a short discussion ensued around the question, What is it? My daughter, who has always had the utmost faith in me, quickly replied: "My dad knows all about it, I'll ask him to come talk to us the next time he visits here." And so it was, some months later, I found myself in this small, jam-packed room with some twelve or thirteen women on their lunch hour, engaged in a lively seminar on the topic, a discussion that actually lasted two hours. I want to thank those women for their generosity, their participation, their curiosity, and their good-will.

NOTES AND REFERENCES

1. Betty Friedan, *The Feminine Mystique* (New York: W. W. Norton and Company, Inc., 1963).

2. Warren Farrell, *The Myth of Male Power* (New York: Simon and Schuster, 1993).

3. Robert Bly, "What Do Men Really Want?" *New Age* (May, 1982), 30 passim 51.

4. Reading, Mass.: Addison Wesley, 1990.

PART I

Background

Chapter 1

Men's Studies, Masculinism, and Science

For better or worse, modern societies embody unrest. How this came about is a long story, beyond the scope of this chapter, but certainly involves the development of enlarged commercial markets, the belief in progress and equality, and the rise of secularism. These elements, when present in society, tend to reduce the sense of organic community, the fate of the whole society within which all individuals feel bound, and undermine the way roles of individuals and groups in folk societies are defined as functionally integrative, according to the traditional myths and stories.

Social movements capture unrest and constitute recurrent phenomena in modern societies since they represent a substantial number of people who feel disenfranchised, alienated, disrespected, oppressed, or in other ways overlooked, discontented, or unfulfilled.

My purpose in this chapter is to deal with some important problems, concepts, and agenda that must be confronted, defined, and formulated if viable men's studies are to emerge. I shall use women's studies as the model and show that men's studies must both define and be defined by 1) an inspirational philosophy (usually associated with a social movement) and 2) the inquiry of science as well as other humanities.

In *Issues in Feminism: A First Course in Women's Studies*, Sheila Ruth states that women's studies has a feminist base.[1] Feminism, though perceived differently by different groups, has some common beliefs, values, and attitudes according to Ruth. These are the valuing of women in themselves as human beings, the belief in the autonomy of women (the right and conditions to control ones own destiny), and the embracement of the (feminine) qualities of compassion, tenderness, and compromise (instead of the "masculine" qualities of aggression, power, and competition). She also asserts that feminists believe women have been denied their rights for centuries and that because myth, fear, and ignorance in the society have produced false and wrong-headed beliefs regarding women, it is necessary for feminists to reject these and affirm women's capacity to be strong, capable, intelligent, successful, and ethical human beings.[2]

Women's study, then, must take on the job, by and for women, of eliminating these biases and fallacies, especially masculinism (the worst sexism), which seeks to put women under the attitudes, standards, and perceptions of men.[3] In short, women must establish women's reality with new aspirations and options. The contributions of women to society in all areas must be discovered and acknowledged. Ruth goes on to allege that since women have been especially prescribed (sometimes burdened) with beauty, tenderness, compassion, and love, and that, since they (women) have been held out on the margins of society (uncorrupted?), now, as they take strategic positions, they (especially feminist women) hold a key to bringing into society matters of human value (in contradistinction to the male warrior values of abusive power and domination). Women's studies also seek to end the war between the sexes, give all people a renewed sense of human worth, and "to affirm in society the quest for harmony, peace, and humane compassion."[4]

Women's study is mainly an intellectual effort, a philosophy, that attempts to endow women with self-respect and correct the fallacies about women. A feminist social movement, then, would, drawing on these principles and studies, implement social changes in society. The two are intimately connected. A social movement concerns the issues of defining key goals, recruiting adherents, and setting up organizational machinery for sustained action since the accomplishment of many goals requires long-term effort. It also involves strategy as to how people in the movement will deal with resistance—peacefully, militantly, or violently. These resistors are often said to be "men in power."

Shortly after the National Organization for Women (NOW) was formed in 1966, some goals were outlined, which included passage of the equal-rights amendment, banning sex discrimination in employment, and instituting childcare programs and childcare tax deduction, maternity leaves, expanded education and job training, and economic assistance for poor women. Other issues such as abortion rights, socialism, lesbianism, and the participation of men in the organization became more controversial.[5] The pattern then is clear: there is movement from unrest to ideological formulation (feminism) to efforts (goals) of social change—from general to particular. Along with efforts of social change, we find another development crucial to our discussion: the correction and production of knowledge, scientific and otherwise—an effort hopefully aligned with the social movement and its goals.

At this point, I'd like to introduce the concept of paradigm.[6] A paradigm refers to a point of view or a frame of reference. In a profound sense, we encounter and see the world only through some paradigm—some sense of *what* it is we see, some interpretation. Culture itself, and the world views and values it embodies, is probably the broadest paradigm. A social movement is a paradigm, too. It's the view that some things are wrong and need to be changed. A paradigm, as a way of seeing (understanding), lets in certain facts and blocks out or neglects others. If I'm thinking of the world as flat, this paradigm discourages me from seeing it as round.

Science, too, may be considered as a way of seeing. In this sense science, most generally, is fashioned in the culture. In our culture it is a way of looking that emphasizes the empirical (that which is said to be knowable *via* observation, sensory faculties, or extension thereof). It also emphasizes an attitude of mind (such as skepticism) and a methodology (for example, designing studies around hypotheses). Since science is part of culture, it also focuses mostly on problems deemed important in the culture or by powerful groups within the culture—for example, to find the conditions correlated with juvenile delinquency so as to most effectively deal with them. These problems are framed in the values or perceptions of the society (for example, the view that parents are to be included in both the focus of the problem and the recommendations following from the study). Undoubtedly, such matters are what Ruth has in mind when she asserts that women's studies have to contend with (even) scientific bias.

Undoubtedly, science has produced much good (in part because in this culture we value "fixing" things that are defined as "broken" or in need of control, as defined in someone's point of view), but the idea that science also embodies points of view can be unsettling to people who view it as the final authority on truth or fact. Because science is embedded in the society, and therefore subject to influences regarding both what it will study and how it will frame (what point of view will be brought to bear on) its topics, and because scientists may themselves unknowingly or consciously, for special interests, omit or emphasize certain data, healthy criticism and vigilance are warranted. For example, a scientist growing up in a society where free-market capitalism is held as a virtue will not likely undertake studies that seriously consider socialist alternatives or that show the harm that can result from instabilities in capitalist business cycles. Yet scientists do sometimes challenge the *status quo* (given truth of the time), and science as an open enterprise may be self-corrective to a degree.

At this point I'd like to coin a new study called "genderology." Strictly speaking, it would discover the general patterns and conditions under which gender develops and changes in individual consciousness as well as the societal circumstances that shape and limit its expression. As long as societies label people "male/female," "boy"/"man," "girl"/"woman" and attach some significance to these labels, genderology has a subject matter—a reason for existence. Another definition of genderology would be the scientific study of the rules, roles, relationships, personalities, and identities, surrounding being male or female in a society.

Genderology (though not called by that name) as a systematic endeavor began recently—around 1960. In sociology, a plethora of text books containing such words in their titles as "men," "women," and "society," or simply "gender in society," appeared. These were ostensibly summaries of the growing scientific knowledge in the field; most were written by women, and some by women who declared their affiliation with feminism at the beginning of their book.[7] Nearly all took a type of conflict paradigm as their guiding point of view. That point of view sees society as an arena in which struggles for power and privilege exist. In a structural sense, it also sees society as bifurcated into some kind of system of oppressors (usually men) and oppressed victims and recommends an activist agenda for reform or revolution, depending on the version of feminism being considered.

We now return to the issue of men's studies. First we need a word for the philosophy, the base of inspiration. There is no perfect word. "Masculinism" will have to do, though there are already so many preconceptions attached to it. Maybe this is good, for this then becomes the challenge. According to Ruth, many such negative assumptions were initially attached to feminine and feminism as well. In general, then, we could say that masculinism seeks dignity and value for all men as human beings. It seeks to celebrate all that is good about men.[8] And the genderology of men would seek to uncover the rules, roles, relationships, personalities, and identities surrounding being male in society. It would seek out the dynamics of growing up male and the structural conditions affecting life chances, amenities, and the varied expressions of being a man.

From an examination of textbooks on gender, it is clear that a genderology of men is needed. Laurel Richardson Walum acknowledges in the preface to her book, used widely in sociology of gender classes, that "the research on the male as a gender category is still so sparse . . . [and the author lacks] experiential knowledge on 'being' and 'doing maleness.'"[9] Other textbook writers have also apparently assumed the subject of gender *is* women's issues. Let me illustrate: Claire M. Renzetti and Daniel J. Curran's book is entitled *Women, Men, and Society*.[10] It is in many ways excellent. Yet some real puzzles show up as I've used it and others in my Sex and Gender in Society classes semester after semester. Contrary to the title, the book carries almost nothing on men. Here's a sampling: the chapter on schools and gender is almost entirely devoted to women's issues—the slow entrance to and the struggles of women historically enrolled in formal education, the tendency to take girls' education less seriously than boys', sexual harassment of girls in school, the math issue (how are women held back on discouraged in math?), and the tendency (changing now) for women to be underrepresented in certain majors (especially those leading to higher-paying jobs) in colleges such as engineering, physics, and other hard sciences or technologies.

The chapter on employment shows the increased number of women in the labor force over the last fifty years and surveys the blockages to good jobs, promotions, and benefits for women. It also shows the women's job ghettos in the economy (areas of work where 80 percent or more of the employees are women, such as in nursing and clerical/secretary) and discusses "double bind" (a term that refers to full-time employed women who also do 60 percent to 90 percent of the housework). The chapter on crime makes quick reference to the fact that most perpetrators and victims are men in our society, and then goes on to discuss such matters as the false allegation that the (small) rises in female perpetrators in some crimes (for example, forgery, embezzlement, and shoplifting) are due to the women's liberation movement; some possible sentencing disparities regarding male and female perpetrators; the problems of rape and pornography; and some possible problems of women's prisons. I do not wish to be misunderstood: I consider all of the above matters as very important—most of them have been neglected for too long, but it is clear that the science of gender from a feminist point of view leaves out some important topics in genderology.

So a big question arises: _What about the men?_ What about boys who outnumber girls in learning disabilities in schools by rates that are five to ten times higher than girls? What about the thousands of men who work in hazardous (dirty, rough, dangerous) jobs? How do the many men who struggle with unemployment, lay-offs, or boring jobs year after year cope? What are the deeper roots of the high crime rates for men? What's it like to be on the lam? To be in prison? To see one's chances for success dwindle to zero especially if a boy comes from the lower classes? What are the multiple sources of the longevity gap between men and women? What amelioration in society would we be doing if women were living shorter lives than men? Do we have any compassion for these men born out of understanding, based on men's studies? Are there any men's studies? Do they deserve to exist?

We would expect resistance to men's studies to come both from some areas within universities and from some segments of the scientific community itself, just as Ruth points out characterized the early stages of feminism and women's studies. One of the issues that will undoubtedly need to be addressed is patriarchy. Patriarchy is often set up as the source of all oppression. Toward the end of Chapter 2, I show how power (often tied to patriarchy) can be seen more analytically, dispassionately, and multifacetedly. Patriarchy is often assumed to be imposed on society only by men, though some exceptions can be found. What is patriarchy? The list varies, but often includes 1) the condition in society where men make most of the key decisions in the political area, 2) the tendency for physical violence, coercion, and war carried out by men, 3) the institutionalization of the "male point of view" or male interests in the society as dominant, or privileged, and 4) the practices of hierarchy.

Questions then arise for men's studies: Is patriarchy always bad? Are all men involved? Should it be considered in some historical, cultural, or geographical context? Do women (or some women) participate in patriarchy? On the other hand, it may be appropriate for men to apologize (and make amends) for the harm of patriarchy and get on with other men's study questions, such as what are the diverse groups of men in society and what are their needs? What are the blockages that prevent poor, addicted, even successful men from fulfilling more of their potential?

Two more issues should be addressed. Firstly, because the viewpoint of science is primarily interested in explanations and generalizations, regarding cause and effect *patterns* in different types of observable phenomena, individual expressions of biography and personal experience have been glossed over. Such have often been thought to be too idiosyncratic, subjective, or particular. Women's studies, nevertheless, brought this type of data into their discipline very significantly. Biographies of contemporary women now abound. In my opinion, men's studies must do the same. Men must speak for themselves, both as human beings and as gendered persons. For this reason I have included the brief autobiography in the next chapter. Men trying to make sense out of their lives as men may find other men's biographies useful. Poetry, plays, songs, and stories are also appropriate.

Secondly, men's studies must be eclectic. We especially must leave room for those disciplines, such as biology or mythology, which suggest that there is something deeper than or unseen by "normal," fashionable social science about being male or female.[11]

In summary, I have attempted to show that men's studies can learn from the model of women's studies. The main goals of science are to accurately describe important phenomena within a delineated scope of observation and to explain the recurrent patterns found. But what is *deemed important* for description and explanation, and from what point of view, is crucial—something outside the realm of science as we often think of it. Those decisions are often made from the point of view of people's beliefs, stereotypes, and preferences, whether benign or political. Men's studies, as it is informed by both masculinism and the associated agenda of a social movement, will guide those decisions. At the same time, both masculinism and science affect and are affected by men's studies. Masculinism must correct wrong-minded ideas about men where they exist, inspire the self-respect of men, and dedicate itself to a vision of a humane society, even one where men make prompt amends.

In conclusion of this section, I would like to illustrate some of the intersections of science, point of view, and gender bias that have been discussed here. The example is domestic violence. Obviously, from a moral standpoint, violence is not desirable. From the point of view of stereotypes, the tendency is to see it as a male-perpetrated phenomena. Afterall, it is assumed that men are larger, more socialized into the acts of combat, more often prone to resort to violence, and that they should be able to protect themselves. Women are more often assumed to be innocent, smaller, more docile, and dependent. A conflict point of view frames the issue as one of perpetrator and victim. From this vantage, the studies were expected to all turn up the same data (facts): men alone are the culprits of domestic violence between spouses. I do not want to excuse the crime of domestic violence: it is abhorrent, shatters the trust people may have had in each other, and sometimes leads to death. What is clear, however, is that, as best as researchers can discover, 1) men may be *underreporting* violence (to authorities) against them from cross-gender intimates as much or more than women, 2) there is a range of abuse from slapping to more serious beatings (with or without a weapon), and 3) that, from surveys, reported violence of women against men *in some parts of the range* may be higher than that of men against women. An almost equal number of women kill men too.[12] This is often said to be in self-defense or retaliation.

What is important here is not necessarily who is to blame, but rather that in my search of the popular press and textbooks, both in introductory sociology and in the sociology of gender, only a segment of the data is highlighted. That segment is the violence of husbands and intimates against women. This can be explained by the fact that only this point of view makes sense, given the stereotypes of men and women that already exist.[13]

In conclusion, I would like to discuss two more topics: 1) other perspectives or points of view for men's studies (besides the conflict approach), and 2) some contemporary men's groups, organizations, and publications.

We have already mentioned the dominance of the conflict perspective in American women's studies, a view that is framed in oppressor–oppressed language. Such a view is especially useful in ferreting out the more subtle and institutionally unquestioned arrangements that disadvantage certain groups in society. The conflict point of view is prevalent in men's studies, as well, especially in looking for the way lack of resources (money, education, or jobs) affect some men's lives, or even how, for example, cultural prescriptions that put men in charge of protecting the society against perceived dangers or encourage beliefs against the abilities of fathers to nurture children, might disadvantage men.

Another salient point of view in sociology is the structural-functional perspective. Here the significance of positive *interdependence* of people and groups in society is emphasized. Men's studies framed in this language would tend, for example, to point to the importance (functions) of men's activities in maintaining families, communities, or societies. The popularity of this point of view has declined to the extent that it assumed that *only* men could carry out these activities (for example, hunting) or that the men's activities deserved higher reward than the women's activities.

The third, and last, point of view that should be mentioned is a combination of critical and interpretative sociology. The former, critical, derives from the tendency of all of us to be absorbed in our culture, that is, to unconsciously carry out its dictates. We seem to be automatons. We do not easily see alternatives, for example, to getting married and having children (at least thirty years ago)—our culture demands it, and we may even personally extol its goodness or propriety. The goal of critical theory is to *expose* the various roots of social control and indoctrination. Lurking in the critical theory agenda there is also an assumption that, once emancipation from unconsciousness is accomplished through this unmasking of arbitrary (cultural) constraints, we can rely on people's goodness and intelligence to create something better. Social movements, even the men's movement, I say, embodies this assumption or hope.

The interpretive perspective, especially on a level of the dynamic interaction of people in everyday life, can be linked to the critical view mentioned above and tends to emphasize the flux and change in life. It is especially useful in noticing choices in peoples' actions, particularly in times of change or in situations where variations from the norm are emerging. I use men's biographies, even my own, here to gain insight into these matters. Indeed, one can see intentional men's groups (see Chapter 9) as providing new meanings and missions for men's lives.[14]

Another (feminist) point of view that is especially strong among some sociologists analyzing gender should be mentioned. It has two points: 1) That we must (usually at the outset) acknowledge the hegemonic white (middle-upper-class) male *system* of privilege, which is institutionalized in the society, and the harm resulting from it to many people—even what this system of privilege costs these white men themselves; and[15] 2) that men's studies must emphasize this point of view (above) so as not to encroach on or dilute women's studies.

A thorough evaluation of all aspects of the above arguments would take us too far afield here. Very briefly, I would note, first, that a structuralist (the system) point of view is certainly legitimate for certain types of analysis—insurance companies do it all the time when predicting rates of death for given cohorts (with certain structural characteristics such as age and sex), irrespective of *which* particular individuals die within the cohort. But, at times, I want to examine the *degree* of structure, what measurements go into the structural characteristics, where and how they operate in the society, and whether they are changing (see my discussion of patriarchy in the next chapter).

The second argument essentially asserts the need to subsume men's studies under women's studies. Of course, I recognize that the development and institutionalization of women's studies involved a struggle and that, also, feminism brought some important new paradigms and analysis into academia. Within this perspective, it is assumed that men's and women's studies are not comparable because, as a whole, women are oppressed more. This point is well expressed by Cramer and Russo: "Men's Studies can be positive [only?] when truly feminist and committed to challenging male power, but too often it focuses on how sex differences limit all of us equally, rather than on sexual inequality and the social significance of men's subordination of women . . . The neutralization of Women's Studies to gender studies is a backlash phenomenon to watch very carefully in the upcoming decade."[16]

Varying points of view, however, can be found, even among academic feminists, on the alleged constancy of oppression on women. Using a social class analysis herself, Hooks asserts that "[Bourgeois white women, especially radical feminists] did not want to acknowledge that . . . though often victimized by sexism [they] have more power and privilege, are less likely to be exploited or oppressed, than poor, uneducated nonwhite males."[17] Finally, let us look at men's groups and publications.

A wide variety of men's groups, organizations, and publications have sprung up since the 1960s, and, especially, since the 1980s. Some of these are local in scope, some national; some are ephemeral and some quite enduring. They range from profeminist men sponsorship to men's-rights sponsors. I do not pretend to take full inventory of them here, but, rather, to give examples. Some of the men's groups come out of a wilderness exploration theme, some from a therapy context, some out of twelve-step recovery work (such as Alcoholics Anonymous), some out of religious groups, some out of academia, and others out of men's-rights advocacy groups.

Profeminist groups of men were among the earliest. Among the largest of these is The National Organization of Men Against Sexism (NOMAS). As the name suggests, these men work primarily for women's (feminist) rights, against inequality, and for the freeing of all society from patriarchy and sexism, especially the sexism of men against women. In their flier we read: "NOMAS advocates a perspective that is pro-feminist, gay-affirmative, anti-racist, and committed to justice on a broad range of social issues including class, age, religion and physical ability. . . . [Though] traditional masculinity includes many positive characteristics . . . [it has also] . . . limited and harmed us . . . As an organization for changing men . . . [we especially work with women against the injustices of] . . . economic and legal discrimination, rape, domestic violence, sexual harassment and many others."[18] *Masculinities*, a national journal, is a joint venture with NOMAS.

The American Men's Studies Association (AMSA) is less explicitly profeminist. Its goals as an association "is to provide a forum for teachers, researchers and therapists to exchange information and gain support for their work with men, . . . [and its intention is] . . . to recognize and respect the many voices emerging from among those working with and/or studying men and masculinity."[19] Those joining AMSA receive the *Journal of Men's Studies*.

Many other journals and newsletters have flourished such as: *The Talking Stick* (Mt. Airy, Maryland), *Men's Reporter* (Madison, Wisconsin), *Men Talk* (Minneapolis-St. Paul), *Mentor* (Portland, Oregon), *Manthem* (Frankenmuth, Michigan), *Man* (Austin, Texas), *The New Warrior Journal* (Milwaukee), and *Wingspan* (formerly from Manchester, Massachusetts, now, LaJolla, California).

Other organizations such as The Coalition of Free Men, The National Congress for Fathers and Children, The American Divorce Association for Men (ADAM), the National Organization for Men, and Fathers for Equal Rights, Inc. have focused their attention on men's rights and discriminations against men such as in custody cases (see my discussion at the end of Chapter 6). Warren Farrell and Herb Goldberg, nationally known authors, have also been active in some of these organizations.

One of the most well-known men's coalitions surrounds its charismatic leader, Robert Bly. This branch of the movement is often called "mythopoetic," a name Bly says doesn't entirely fit. Bly's appearance on Public Broadcasting with Bill Moyers in the presentation of "A Gathering of Men" galvanized, more than any other single event, grassroots interest in men and the men's movement. Bly's message derives, in large part, from some old liberating and confrontational stories for men from mythology, his knowledge of men in other cultures, and his keen sensitivity to the demise of the "male spirit" in modern (industrial) times. Furthermore, he faces squarely the many sources and effects of shame on men and the various sources of grief in men's lives (see Chapter 8). There is no ongoing mythopoetic men's organization as such (though there are retreats), and much of the published writing, videos, and cassettes in this vain are announced in a newsletter (*Dragonsmoke*) and sold through the Minneapolis-based Ally Press Center.[20]

In closing, I would like to add a personal note of caution about categorizing men in various men's groups. Recently, a woman acknowledged her husband to me, saying that "I'm glad he's not like all the rest of those men out there." I know she had good intentions in her heart, but something in me called out against her remark because, I say, we men are all in the *same* boat. The notion that there are just a few good men out there sounds both spurious and devisive to me. Yes, I know some men rape women, but some men *don't*. We all have our shadows (see Chapter 8). Furthermore, I know from a spiritual standpoint that I'm not enlightened unless *you* are too. That's just the way it works. We shall *all* gather in Zion. If we draw the lines solidly, and I hope we don't, between "us" (the few good men) and "them"

(for example, abusive men), we're in deep trouble—the men's movement is over, and I'm going home. We must reach out more and more
and more to *all* men (even, and here's one of the challenges for me, to
the *pro*feminist, "intellectual" men). I stand for the honor of *all* men
and for the possibility of our blessing *all* women as well, especially
those who seek to divide us into the good men and the bad men.

NOTES AND REFERENCES

1. Boston: Houghton Mifflin Co., 1980, 4.
2. Ruth, 4.
3. Ruth, 7.
4. Ruth, 9.
5. See Joyce Gelb and Marian Lief Palley, *Women and Public Policies*
(Princeton, N.J.: Princeton University Press, 1982), 30–31.
6. See Earl R. Babbie, *Sociology* (Belmont, Calif.: Wadsworth Publishing Company, 1983), 615–616.
7. For example, see Laurel Richardson Walum, *The Dynamics of Sex
and Gender* (Boston: Houghton Mifflin, 1981), ix.
8. For example, see Warren Farrell, *Why Men Are the Way They Are*
(New York: McGraw-Hill, 1986), 287–308.
9. Richardson, ix.
10. Boston: Allyn and Bacon, 1992.
11. For another definition of men's studies, narrower than mine, see
Harry Brod, *The Making of Masculinities* (Winchester, Mass.: Allen and
Unwin, 1987).
12. R. L. McNeely and Gloria Robinson-Simpson, "The Truth About
Domestic Violence: A Falsely Framed Issue," *Social Work* 32 (November-
December, 1987), 485–490. Also, see the very interesting article by Mal-
colm J. George, "Riding The Donkey Backwards: Men as the Unacceptable
Victim of Marital Violence," *The Journal of Men's Studies* 3 (November,
1994), 137–159. For a somewhat different point of view, see Demie Kurz,
"Social Science Perspective on Wife Abuse: Current Debates and Future
Directions," *Gender and Society* 3 (December, 1989), 489–505.
13. Of course, what is recommended is a multi-perspectivalist approach,
which would allow us to notice violence in the dyad on the part of *either*
spouse (or, for example, between parents and children), but my point here
is that, when preexisting beliefs exist (for example, that women are not

capable of certain types of violence), it is more unlikely that the female to male violence will be noticed or taken as significant.

14. These perspectives can be found in various sociology texts, for example, see Ruth A. Wallace and Allison Wolf, *Contemporary Sociological Theory* (Englewood Cliffs, N.J.: Prentice-Hall, 1995).

15. See, for example, Joseph H. Pleck, "Men's Power with Women, Other Men, and Society: A Men's Movement Analysis," in Michael S. Kimmel and Michael A. Messner, eds., *Men's Lives* (New York: Macmillan, 1992), 19–27. The implication here is a familiar one: that in the system most men are powerless, and that this powerlessness is one of the prime reasons men dominate women.

16. Patricia Cramer and Ann Russo, "Toward a Multicentered Women's Studies in the 1990's" in Cheris Kramarae and Dale Spender, eds., *The Knowledge Explosion: Generations of Feminist Scholarship* (New York: Teachers College Press, 1992), 99–117. The quote is from p. 106, and the insert is mine.

17. Bell Hooks, "Men: Comrades in Struggle," in Laura Kramer, ed., *The Sociology of Gender* (New York: St. Martin's Press, 1991), 487–499. (Quote is on p. 488.)

18. National Organization for Men Against Sexism, Suite 300, 54 Mint Street, San Francisco, California 94103.

19. American Men's Studies Association, 22 East Street, Northampton, Massachusetts 01060.

20. For an early sense of the need for and benefits of a men's movement, see my (Clinton Joyce Jesser) "Oh My Loving Brother," *M. Gentlemen for Gender Justice* 6 (Fall, 1981), 16, 17. More references to men's centers, councils, and publications can be found in the back of Christopher Harding, ed., *Wingspan: Inside The Men's Movement* (New York: St. Martin's Press, 1992), 253–264. Also, see: The Men's Health Network (310 D Street, N.E., Washington, D.C. 20002); The Changing Men Collections, Michigan State University Libraries, East Lansing, Michigan 48824-1048; Eugene R. August, *The New Men's Studies: A Selected and Annotated Interdisciplinary Bibliography*. 2d ed. (Englewood, Colo.: Libraries Unlimited, Incorporated, 1994); San Femiano, ed. *Men's Studies Syllabi*, 11th ed. (22 East Street, Northampton, Mass., 01060).

Chapter 2

Gender, Society, and Gender History

As society changes so does our awareness of salient identities. This is especially true with regard to gender. Fifty years ago gender was addressed very little. True, we have always had our folkwisdom regarding men and women, previous women's movements have struggled for legal and economic equality, and, from the beginning, in surveys, we asked or checked off the box containing "sex": _____ male or_____ female; _____ man or _____ woman. Still, as long as family and kinship units remained large or stable, little investigation as to the nature and development of gender seemed important.[1] A few studies appeared now and then on men's or women's lives, but these were not consistently connected with concerns over power or issues in the life-course, nor were they systematically tied to changes in society and its institutions.

All this changed in the 1960s or before. The birth rate, except for the short-term rise in the 1950s, continued to fall; urbanization and the creation of jobs continued to grow; inflation rose; consumer demands expanded; mass education, even at the college level, grew for both men and women; longevity kept going up; both the age at first marriage and divorce rates rose as the size of the family unit shrank; female employment increased dramatically; and ambitious desires for personal liberty and individual rights, whether one be male or female, black or white, emerged with new vigor.

r, the boy/girl, man/woman label and its expectations,
: in its own right, and many new scholarly journals
:nder concerns appeared.[2] Gender was now a more
central life interest, a key feature of identity anchored to more gen-
der-conscious groups and groupings. Gender ideology, with concerns
for status and power, bloomed. By ideology I mean the ideas generated
by various interest groups about what is a woman and what is a man,
about the proper means of raising boys and girls in society, and the
proper roles and rewards assigned to each in the life course and in the
central institutional activities of the society.

Ideology assumes what men's and women's needs are, their plastic-
ity, their importance, and their deeper natures. Where there are felt
deprivations, ideologies often ferret out their cause, and, in the case
of social movements such as reforms or revolutions, lay out a blueprint
and strategy for correction or for reaching a more just state of affairs.
Other ideologies also defend the *status quo*; they counterpose the social
movement with often elaborate justifications as to why things are best
left the way they are. Often they are the boxes given to us within which
dialogue for change can take place.

Gender can be seen as both related to and independent of sex
(male/female). The development in biological make-up seems to be
fairly clear. Life begins with conception, and that usually from a
successful coital act between a fertile female and a fertile male partner.[3]
The male ejaculate contains some ratio of gynosperms (usually 22 +
X chromosomes) and androsperms (usually 22 + Y chromosomes).
Because the androsperm is smaller and swims faster, it has a slightly
better chance of fertilizing the female egg (usually 22 + X chromosomes), especially if intercourse takes place very close to ovulation in
the female since that is the period in her cycle when the alkaline
character of the cervix best allows androsperms entrance and survival.

In this case (a 44 + XY conception), a number of physiological
differentiations normally develop in the growth of the embryo-be-
coming-a-fetus, to bring about, or set in place for later, the development of male characteristics such as primary (penis and testes for
example) and secondary (for example, facial hair, voice change, and
ejaculations) sex characteristics. These are some of the essentials that

go into the label called "sex," and many of these characteristics would seem to be geared to the specific needs and roles of procreation later: males take an active part in fertilizing, females in conceiving and carrying the pregnancy. The extent to which different roles in courtship or sexual signaling are believed to occur between human adult males and females, and the extent to which they are hormonally imprinted or instinctual, is more complex and controversial.

What other differences separate the sexes, how large are they, and how important are they in socially organized life? These are big and debatable questions compounded by the fact that if we look for differences, we find them or create them. Early on, females seem to have more highly developed sensory acuity (in sight, hearing, touch). They also tend to take the lead in fine-motor coordination of the body as infants. Other things being equal, females seem to be more resistant to early life-threatening diseases. Thus, the surplus of male births over female begins to even out within fifteen to twenty years, and because of a continuing higher male death rate, female life expectancy outdistances male life expectancy after that. After puberty, there also appear to be some strength, speed, and performance differences between the sexes, other factors being equal.

There also appear to be genetic-hormonally based differences between the sexes in general perceptual/cognitive functions as well as early (and persistent) differences in agitation, reactions to being physically confined, roughness in interpersonal contact and play (all higher for males) and, later, relational affinity to others. (This last claim centers on speculations that females have greater concern over the impact of actions on the *web* of social relations while males have greater proclivities for *hierarchy* or social distance).[4]

Anywhere earlier, you might have been asking, But what of the way infants are *treated* (by adults) once we label them boy or girl from day one? And you would have been right in asking or protesting that I've left this out. Nature and nurture occur together. Society (nurture) is already at work. We're already polarized with conceptions of and definite roles for boy and girl; we're already given to ideologies and beliefs about gender before the child is born. In short, we attempt to teach children their gender based on our determination of their sex and on our beliefs as to what is appropriate for that sex.

What we can see is what—if the sex of the fetus in the uterus has not already been disclosed—everyone present at birth is waiting to announce. And so they do, and gender becomes a very pervasive identity. The neonate[5] is guided toward a gendered person—masculine or feminine—by means of a huge array of supports, directions, messages, and rewards. We give the child a gendered name (for example, John or Jane), clothes, room furnishings, and toys all depending on his or her sex. We hold, stroke, speak to him or her in different ways, reading certain stories, play particular games, visualize different futures, set male and female models before the child, and reward their appropriate emulation. This is a large part of what is called socialization. And so, sociologists, social psychologists, developmental psychologists, and educators of all sorts study these supports and messages, discern their consequences, and follow boys and girls, men and women, and their groups throughout the life cycle, from the womb to the tomb. These are very useful and legitimate areas of inquiry. Reflection on this indoctrination can even be liberating to a person. It gives us a sense of how we are shaped.

Another very important concern for us is gender history (or prehistory) and the functional relation of gender and sex to society. This is no insignificant concern since our sense of both identity and dignity is reflected in how our history is told or written. Whoever wields the pen holds some power. One's version of history is connected to one's ideology. Of special interest here is the question of whether or not there might be some larger plan or set of exigencies in the service of which gender socialization occurs or has occurred up to this time in most human societies. In other words, the question is: Do we find throughout the world that, because of differences in biology between males and females or simply because of convenience, some different functions for men and women cut across the diverse societies of earth? This is a big and very important question.

One of the most ambitious attempts to answer it is David D. Gilmore's recent study, *Manhood in the Making: Cultural Concepts of Masculinity*,[6] and his answer is yes. Yes, especially when human societies face scarcity and the need for internal or external protection in the face of danger. The survival strategy most societies use is to put their men most at risk. This includes almost all human societies where economic adaptation requires facing some significant hazards away from the hearth, for example, big-game hunting, heavy construction, fishing in treacherous waters—it also pertains to the preservation of an internal order, defense against external enemies or the encroachment of strangers, or the deployment of men when expansion of the group by conquering others is undertaken. (Women, incidentally, are more at risk of death due to childbearing.) In other words, making a living requires effort, and the danger of losing what has been gained by the group or its expansion into larger territories usually requires some hierarchies of control and protection among and by men.[7]

In these societies masculinity often requires a selfless sacrifice of men for the larger and long-term good of the group. Men are thus raised to show a readiness to act forcefully and daringly for the welfare of the group and, in so doing, to put their own lives in jeopardy. Presumably, timidity isn't an option. In this way we can say they display their nurturance too. In this process of socialization, boys are taught to deny their dependence (that is, on mother) so as to be dependable to the group and to suppress their fear of danger in order to serve others.

Of course, this has a price. Fears, insecurities, and dependencies cannot be completely suppressed. They are an integral part of life and human existence. Unless they are acknowledged and expressed occasionally under safe conditions, they emerge distorted as toxic masculinity: as cruelty, rage,[8] or overdomination. This is part of our topic in Chapter 4.

What has happened in history as fact, or of what significance men's roles have been to society, are certainly contested topics. New historians revise history and so change our conceptions of the past. By and large, feminist writers have dissented from simplistic views of survival of the toughest or views that seem to downplay the centrality of mother-infant bonds and the contributions of *women's* labor and innovations to society and culture. (See Evaluation section at the end of this chapter.)

This division of labor between the sexes, which often places men in the aggressive and protective mode in the face of danger, Farrell calls Stage I survival.[9] Historically, men were required to be killers (of animals or enemies) in order to be protectors (of women and children). This was necessary for survival of the fittest, when fighting for food and water was the focus of life. Farrell calls this a Stage I society.

Farrell feels that once a society has a substantial number of people who do not need to worry about dying of starvation, it can move into Stage II, characterized by a balance between survival and self-fulfillment. He says that in Stage II, training men to be killers no longer leads to the survival of the fittest, but rather, with nuclear technology, to the potential destruction of everyone. He warns, though, that we are still training men to be killed in work and in war in order to protect us—that 94 percent of the people dying at work are men, and more than 99 percent of the people dying at war are still men. The problem with continuing to rely on men to be killer/protectors is that it desensitizes men from being nurturer/connectors.

Men also need connectiveness, with safe emotional releases, and the supports for development and enhancement of their personal well-being over the whole life course (See Chapter 9). Furthermore, it is a big mistake, Farrell suggests, to look back on earlier societies from *today's* (Stage II) standards. In so doing we condemn men for acting badly. What is fairer to say is that they were often behaving appropriately to their times and conditions.

For the most part, I am going to avoid the terms "masculine" and "feminine" for several reasons. Though they are real to people as far as messages or expectations communicated to boys and girls (boys/girls don't do that), they are culturally defined (vary from society to society) and may be quite vague as well. Many writers on men, especially in sociology, talk about the male value system (strong, independent, dominant, aggressive, forceful, unemotional) as if men were automatons—that by simply knowing these (vague) values (or personality traits) we then know (can assume) how men act—we don't even have to go out and observe or let men speak for themselves. This is assumed to be masculinity in the United States, and it's often spoken of as *the* problem for men. What I see, however, in our world, are messages and situations where we constantly negotiate, pick up cues, turn, twist, bend, improvise in regard to expectations for our actions. We also make unpopular choices from time to time and pay the price of acting "unmasculine."10

Another problem with the supposition of the masculine value system is the tendency to come out from our selective observations with only a *caricature* of men—a picture that fits the value system, but ignores the other qualities or behaviors of men. For example, one of the excellent characteristics of Osherson's work with men (Chapter 4) is his sensitivity to real men in real situations (speaking for themselves). If, for example, we assume men are nonintimate (usually measured against a standard or styles of intimacy fitting women or some segment of women), then we are not likely to even see the stylized manifestations of closeness men might exhibit, or their struggle to close any gap they may sense between their desired and actual levels of intimacy as Osherson does.

It's also interesting that, in Oriental philosophy, there is yin (feminine) and yang (masculine). For example, receptive is feminine and giving is masculine, while hot and cold are also labelled masculine and feminine. What's more useful here, in my opinion, is that there is no *preference* for the one over the other, but, rather, the view that the one needs or compliments the other, and that actual men and women have *both*. Thus, the title of this book, Fierce *and* Tender Men.

Also, often, reference to masculine and feminine simply complicates things. We might as well talk about the behavior *per se* (directly) rather than talk about the behavior and then add that it is masculine or feminine. Recently, I heard two psychotherapists presenting their work with men and sexual addictions, and they kept talking about these from the standpoint of masculine behavior. When someone in the audience asked them why not call them simply learned or adaptive (but inappropriate, illegal or damaging) behavior? they had no good answer except to say that the clients themselves sometimes referred to being a man (and presumably to the model of behavior they felt that required).

Finally, seemingly to counter my own argument, but on a deeper level, I have a hunch that there may be something about the male or female members of a species—even the human species—that comes from nonconscious programming. Social scientists are generally averse to this idea, but transpersonal and biological investigators, who look for this programming, will not be easily silenced. In other words, there may be something "imaginal" and/or biological that inclines (not determines) us as men and women toward certain modalities such as defense or nest-making. Is it *essential* to male and female? I don't know. Must it be fulfilled in males and females in a *particular* way? I don't think so. Is it modifiable? Definitely.[11]

EVALUATION

I will concentrate here mainly on the evaluation of some questions that arise concerning power in this chapter.

As indicated in the preface, inequality has become one of the key issues between the sexes in our society. In this chapter, too, considerations of inequality were lurking in discussions of upbringing (Should girls, for example, be raised toward more aggressiveness and higher aspiration?) or defense (Should risky masculine tasks be more rewarded?). The underlying factor is power (and prestige). What is the nature of power? Is it multifaceted? Yes.

Traditionally, sociologists have thought about power largely in terms of resources that are easily measured or transferred within the society, for example, wealth or assets for which there is a demand. Other indicators are the ability to determine outcomes in various realms of decision-making (including politics), as well as achieved occupational and educational levels. Also, there is the use of superior weapons and physical force. Often overlooked, though, are control of or influence in the idea-producing system (for example, religion or mythology, which often provides a sort of rationale for who should rule or get what rewards) as well as virtuousness, charm, good looks, and persuasiveness, although the latter are more person attached and not necessarily transferable to one's descendants. We might even add empowerment (for example, the enhancement of others, as in good parenting).

The application to male-female relations seems quite straight forward: Do men have more wealth in their name (control) than women? Greater longevity? More skills and education (especially in fields where more prestige or money can be earned)? Higher representation in politics? Are they seen as more virtuous and honest? More worthy of assistance?

How about the comparison in power between men and women across societies? Here, new complications arise since societies differ over a broad continuum in size, technology, and productivity from a small hunting-gathering society to a large industrial society. Also, there is the tendency to divide women's and men's activity into separate realms, for example, women to interior tasks and men to exterior tasks. Can separate be equal? Not withstanding these caveats, some generalizations can be made in regard to the conditions that tend to enhance power and status. As a change of pace I will express these in the interests of women. They are[12]: 1) female involvement in food-production—food supply is adequate and reliable—and women's participation in the bartering or sale of food and goods; 2) shared child-rearing with men after the initial stage of intensive mother-infant care is over; 3) matrilineal kinship reckoning (through the mother's line); 4) matri-local marriage patterns (where residence is established in the wife's locale or village after marriage, or where the spouses stay in their separate villages while married as among the Ashanti of Nigeria); 5) equality of inheritance to both spouses or to both female and male children; 6) literacy (and coveted specialized training); 7) access to effective contraception; 8) peacefulness in the society (low militarism); and 9) significant input from women in politics and the idea-production spheres.

Since unilateral or complete dominance of one sex over the other in society is not possible, we might not use the word "matriarchy" even in the best of combinations above. There is always some balance of power.

One can also see how even these more specific conditions may be interconnected or require supporting conditions. For example, contraception is not likely to be an issue if death rates in the society are high; and the latter (death rates) are likely to be high where food production (in relation to the population) and the amenities of life are low (such as sanitation and medical care) or where warfare or natural disasters regularly kill large numbers of people. Correlatively, patriarchy also becomes a more complicated matter.

Finally, I want to comment on the bias sometimes found against men in what is called structural (liberal) sociology especially the version that often uses only wealth and politics as indications of power. One of the most widely used books on men's lives in academic sociology is Clyde W. Franklin II's *Men and Society*.[13] In many respects it is a fine work. He says: "One *has* to refer to male dominance qualities of *America's social structure* rather than individual men's sexist qualities."[14] He goes on to note that social structure exists at the level of organizations (for example, athletic programs), institutions (for example, jobs in the economy), and culture (for example, customs and literature). Fine, I have no problem with that as analytical analysis. But he (and others) then speak of this structure as *constraining* people's behavior.[15]

Further, he states, "A basic thesis here is that, in America, sex refers to ascribed characteristics which can ultimately determine one's social position in the social structure. In our society, if a person is born male he *automatically* enjoys a higher social position relative to a person who is born female."[16] This is a bit overstated in my opinion, and, in some cases, it is flatly false as, for example, when we compare "Happy" Rockefeller (an upper-class woman) with Willie Horton (a lower-class black man convicted of crimes).

Finally, Franklin concludes that today American society "is beset with social problems: hunger, destructive competition between its members, violent aggression between racial and ethnic groups, sexual exploitation of women, intergroup prejudice and discrimination, child abuse, wife abuse, and in general, dysfunctional living patterns, basically *promulgated by men*."[17] What can we say? Is this a careful, reasoned analysis that we would expect from seeing society as a conjoint creation with intricate interdependencies, or is this simply sloppy "blame-making?" In conclusion, I am not saying that social structure or masculinity or femininity prescriptions do not shape our lives, but what I am saying is that this analysis must seek out variations from the patterns and must be anchored in accounts from men speaking for themselves from the point of view of *their* own lives and the way they actually deal with masculine expectations, especially in times of change.[18] The next chapter (an autobiography) represents such an account.

Another critical view of men is espoused by Michael S. Kimmel in sociology. In my opinion it is distorted, but it does seem to receive a lot of attention as a men's study perspective. Two assertions dominate Kimmel's viewpoint: 1) That men are in the men's movement primarily because they are confused or in crises with masculinity, and that is because they (these middle-aged, middle-class, white, heterosexual men) are losing power and privilege in a society that has increasingly become urbanized, industrialized, and secularized.[19] These men are just *reactive* in Kimmel's view, trying to hang onto or reclaim their superordinate power. 2) That initiation as well as other men's work suffers from a *rejection* of the feminine, that is, *too much* emphasis on separation of men from mothers. "Manhood [in these men's groups] is defined as a flight from femininity . . ."[20] which Kimmel believes is wrong. (He adores femininity—his version—in the abstract.)

My own view is that masculinity is often constructed (by critics such as Kimmel) as a caricature—a straw-man if you will. Also, Kimmel displays a fundamental misunderstanding of masculinity in a large part of the men's movement especially with reference to the warrior (or wildman). First, these are not to be taken as literal men, but rather (see Chapter 8) as energies or metaphors. The Warrior in the many groups in which I have participated is not regarded as a savage killer, but rather represents focused energy (in the service of a noble mission), accountability, integrity, *and* the embracement of *one's own feminine*. It is also a look into our own shadows and shortcomings.[21]

The real question I have of Kimmel's recent writings concerns his ethnographic method. Loosely speaking, ethnography is the study of culture from the participant's point of view. Usually, an ethnographer describes the customs and values of a group being observed. Ethnography has a strong tradition in sociology. While a researcher need not agree with the goodness of the everyday life being observed, some level of *respect* is appropriate. Kimmel states that his (and co-author Kaufman's) attendance at men's events occurred "over a variety of retreats and conferences in various parts of the United States."[22] Kimmel seems to be trying to tell on men without them finding out. Several questions arise: What were the authors' roles there at these men's retreats and conferences? Did they share with the other men at the beginning of these events their reason for being there? Was confidentiality and good faith upheld? Did the authors' presuppositions override what they were willing to learn with these men? Who specifically said what, for example, that their masculinity and privilege were threatened or that they hated their mothers? If comments of this type were made at the men's gathering, what was their broader context? Were the authors ever in an ongoing mythopoetic or new-warrior men's group? Would the authors go back to these men's groups and let the men actually read the account they had written and published about them? Is this pop journalism masquerading as professional sociology?[23]

I invite you now to shift gears. The background of this chapter has been in effect, our lives writ large, that is, it has involved considerations that set the parameters to some extent for gender development and gender debate in our society. The next chapters turn to areas of men's gendered lives, intersected by culture and personal experience, to our infancy and early childhood, to sex, fatherhood and work, play and healing.

NOTES AND REFERENCES

1. Only a short (four pages) and very interesting discussion on "Sex Differences" by Albert Moll occurs in Robert E. Park and Ernest W. Burgess's *Introduction to The Science of Sociology* (Chicago: University of Chicago Press, 1921), 88–92. The viewpoint expressed definitely leans toward the role of nature, that is, that there are physically determined interests—rough games for boys, doll and nurse games for girls—that separate the sexes due to their natures.

2. For example: *Feminist Issues; Gender and Society; Genders; Journal of Women and Aging; Psychology of Women Quarterly; Sex Roles; Signs; Women*

and Health; Women and Politics; Women's Studies International Quarterly.
Others, more popular, are *Ms., Self, Working Woman,* and *Lears.*

3. Kenneth S. Jones, Louis W. Shainberg, and Curtis O. Byer, *Sex* (New York: Harper, 1969). Also, see Corinne Hutt, *Males and Females* (Baltimore: Penguin Books, 1972).

4. See, for example, Carol Gilligan, *In a Different Voice* (Cambridge, Mass.: Harvard University Press, 1982).

5. The unsocialized infant.

6. New Haven, Conn.: Yale University Press, 1990.

7. Steve Smith, "Men: Fear and Power," *Men's Studies Review* 8 (1992), 20–27. In general, we can also say when a number of people have to be mobilized quickly to respond to emergencies (for example, a firefighting group), a hierarchical structure through which commands are issued is needed. There isn't time to sit around and take a vote.

8. Rage is anger that wants to spill over out of any container put around it. Also see Chapter 9, regarding anger.

9. Warren Farrell, *The Myth of Male Power* (New York: Simon & Schuster, 1993).

10. At the end of Chapter 4, I refer to a family background survey I sometimes take from students in my classes. This includes the number and gender of older and younger siblings. What caught my eye as I read these were the many references to gender-atypical socialization in terms of the playthings (hand-me-downs) especially if the child had an older cross-gender sibling. There were numerous reports of girls playing with trucks and boys playing with dolls. Also, there were many reports of daughters going fishing or playing ball with fathers, and (perhaps fewer) sons helping moms. Along these lines, see Tracey Idle, Eileen Wood, and Serge Desmaroes, "Gender Role Socialization in Toy Play Situation: Mothers and Fathers with Their Sons and Daughters," *Sex Roles* 28 (June, 1993), 679–691, especially their summarization: ". . . [There is] a change in parents' perception of what is acceptable gender-typing behavior," 679. Also see Kaj Bjorkquist, "Sex Differences in Physical, Verbal and Indirect Aggression: A Review of Recent Research," *Sex Roles* 30 (February, 1994), 177–184, where he states ". . . it is nonsensical to claim that males are more aggressive than females," 177.

11. See Janis S. Bohan, "Regarding Gender: Essentialism, Constructionism and Feminist Psychology," *Psychology of Women Quarterly* 17 (March, 1993), 5–21.

12. I have abstracted these generalizations from various sources. Two that were especially helpful were: Helen Mayer Hacker, "Gender Roles from a Cross-Cultural Perspective," in Lucile Duberman, *Gender and Sex in Society* (New York: Praeger, 1975), 185–215 and Pierre L. van den Berghe, *Age and Sex in Human Societies: A Biosocial Perspective* (Belmont, Calif.: Wadsworth, 1973).

13. Chicago: Nelson-Hall, 1988.

14. Franklin III, (emphasis mine), 53.

15. Franklin III, (emphasis mine), 54.

16. Franklin III, (emphasis mine), 57.

17. Franklin III, (emphasis mine), 82.

18. It's quite obvious that some research on this topic fails to distinguish between *different* questions: 1) What do men *do* (where, when, with whom)? 2) What do men (or others) *say* men do? 3) What do men (or others) say they *should* do?

19. Michael S. Kimmel and Michael Kaufman, "Weekend Warriors: The New Men's Movement," in Harry Brod and Michael Kaufman, eds., *Theorizing Masculinities* (Thousand Oaks, Calif.: Sage Publications, 1994), 259–288.

20. Kimmel and Kaufman, 271.

21. See "The New Warrior Training Adventure" brochure available from 2604-A North Lake Drive, Milwaukee, Wisc. 53211. Also, see the excellent discussion: Francis Shor, "Contrasting Images of Reconstructing Manhood: Bly's Wild Man Versus Spielberg's Inner Child," *The Journal of Men's Studies* 2 (November, 1993), 109–128.

22. Kimmel and Kaufman, 263.

23. If I am proven wrong in how I have characterized either Franklin's or Kimmel's views here, I shall, in the spirit of the warrior, promptly apologize to them directly.

PART II

In the Men's Houses

Chapter 3

"Clinton, I Hardly Knew Ye"[1]: An Autobiographical Journey

Anyone can benefit from writing an autobiography. It's an especially important task here because, if written in honesty, autobiography is sure to connect us with our journey and the larger context of society in which are lives are situated. The autobiography lets people speak for themselves and can also help the reader see where (and how) personal experience or background affect one's ideas.

My life began on a small, rented, subsistence farm in central North Dakota on the day of my birth: Thanksgiving Day, November 28, 1934. That was in the Depression, and times were hard. I'm told that I was a blue baby— not breathing at birth—lain aside for dead. But somehow I survived. I was the youngest of two, my brother being two years older.

My father came from a large farm family and he was nearly illiterate. My mother took to "book learning" much more readily and she pushed my brother and me away from farming and toward education. I remember nothing in my life until I was five years old, lying in bed stricken by diphtheria, rubbing my legs hard against each other because they ached. Again, I wasn't expected to live. But I did.

In school I was a pretty good student. A few teachers (mostly women) went the extra mile for me. In childhood, I remember good times and bad times. Inwardly I worried a lot, but hardly ever told anyone what I was dwelling on. Life in North Dakota on a farm, especially in the winter, seemed very precarious. We didn't have electricity or running water until I was about twelve years old. Outwardly, I was often recalcitrant: Me scared?—not me, I'll show 'em! On a number of occasions I got some very severe whippings from my dad.

Because of the gulf between our education and the times, I was not close to my father. I worked with him, but we never played together. The fact that my mother was especially proud of my brother's and my accomplishments in school, and somewhat resentful that my father did not have these, strained our family.

Because my brother was older and stronger when a division of labor was needed, I sometimes stayed in the house or around the farmstead to help my mother inside or outside with chores, while he went out to the field to help my father. I was probably her darling (which is a tough place for a little boy to be). Though she was often sick, my mother worked very hard when she was on her feet, sometimes on the hayrack or shoveling grain. Sometimes I tried to take care of her when she was ill. I, too, was sick a lot of the time, but my health improved considerably after puberty and my tonsillectomy at age sixteen. Even today at age sixty, at 150 pounds, I'm a small man, something I don't like to admit. In my stubbornness or determination, I held my own—even excelled—in sports or active games up until high school. I tried my damnedest after that, too, but with less success. I've stayed in some kind of physical conditioning regimen—jogging, martial arts, calisthenics, yoga—all my life.

My connection with my mother was deeper and she ran the show, but I must tell one story for my father. Winters in North Dakota were often harsh, the roads undeveloped, and the snow deep. Several times in these conditions, at my mother's urging, my father hitched our two horses to a small, open sleigh with eight to ten inches of straw on the floor. My brother and I lay on the straw, my father threw two or three big quilts over us, and off we'd go toward town. It was snugly under there, and I could feel the sled sway and hear the runners creak as they glided over the deep, dry snowdrifts. Somewhere along the five-mile trip to Turtle Lake, I'd peek out from under our coverings and see my father standing tall, dressed in a big winter cap and overcoat, holding the reins and steadfastly looking ahead while the very cold wind and snow swirled in his face. On at least one occasion, his face had frozen in spots by the time we reached town. The horses almost seemed to know where to go by themselves. They were heroes, too, when in the low draws they encountered snow so deep it suspended them temporarily at the belly, preventing their hooves from touching ground. All this to see that we got to school.

I had my first girlfriend around age eight. (I was an early starter.) I had at least eight or ten more "close" girlfriends on through high school. I liked to play at (serial) monogamy. Relationships have always told me a lot about myself, whether I like it or not.

The other thing that was big in my life was religion. We were Baptists. That involved a lot of don'ts: drink, smoke, premarital sex—don't even use scissors on Sunday. I spent a lot of time in church and Sunday school—even Wednesday night prayer service when we'd all kneel (without cushions) and everyone spoke aloud simultaneously. What a din of voices that was. It sometimes lasted twenty minutes, and you didn't get up until the last person finished. That was usually an older man in the back of the church praying in German and weeping his heart out.

As is probably true for other farm children, various events gradually took me out into the larger world, especially during high school, and then to college. Breaking away from home and our small community was somewhat exciting, but not easy. Instead of going to seminary after completing my bachelor's degree as I had planned—I was a heretic in most theological arguments anyway— almost by accident, I got an assistantship and started graduate school in sociology. This was challenging, exciting, and hard work. As a student I was harsh in my criticism of other academicians' work, especially of men's writings, but I did not understand this at the time. For my master's degree, one dear professor sent me to live on the deeply impoverished Pine Ridge Indian Reservation in South Dakota in the summer of 1957, so I could collect standard-of-living data for him and work toward my thesis on cultural conflict and religion among the Teton Dakota, Ogllala Sioux. I would later understand the energy of this professor to be King energy (see Chapter 8), but the experience was cultural shock through and through.

Even years after we'd completed our monograph on Sioux religion, I was still very naive as to what its deeper significance was. For example, about fifteen years after the book, I met Selo Black Crow when he came to Northern Illinois University where I am currently employed. This was at the peak of the 1973 occupation of Wounded Knee on the Pine Ridge Reservation. What moved me deeply was his prayer for all people, including the FBI (his foes), and of praise for the spirits of the wind, rain, fire, thunder, plants, mountains, and all living creatures. It was truly soul speaking.

After my stay on Pine Ridge, I got married, finished a doctoral program in sociology and anthropology, and started into my career at the pace of about sixty-five hours per week in university teaching, research, and writing. I viewed this in part as being a good provider. Ours was a dual-career marriage almost from the beginning, though there was some agreement that mine should take precedence. We had two children and a lot of tensions trying to get all the jobs done (isolated from extended family) and trying to find some of that personal satisfaction we have all come to expect in modern marriage. I was anxious to earn tenure, higher salary, and, in general, climb the ladder.

Marriage and family experts tell us of two critical curves that evolve during a marriage. One is the demands-on-time-and-energy curve early in the marriage, especially when children arrive, and, the other, the income curve, which, hopefully, often rises (more slowly) and may even hit its peak only *after* the children reach early adulthood.

What I now notice is: 1) that I am grateful for being paid a salary for what I mostly like to do (not many people can say that); 2) that marriages such as ours had few guidelines—an almost constant and often painful renegotiation was needed on what was equitable and respectful for a partnership, especially with feminist philosophy rapidly emerging; 3) that I was, or made myself, very isolated—I had few close friends and no best male friends at all;[2] and 4) that, though I was successful, I increasingly found myself both dissatisfied and needy (more was never enough)—as to what might be missing, I had no clue. I hardly noticed that I'd left home, my parents were aging, and I hadn't done any deep grieving work. I didn't know me.

On December 14th, 1973, I faced one of my most profound learning experiences. I walked into the hospital room in Bismarck, North Dakota, where my father was dying. When my mother called to ask me to come—and when I left Illinois—I saw this trip as an inconvenience, but it was much more than that. I had, after all, a huge end-of-the-semester bundle of term papers under my arm. For three excruciating days and nights, I stood by his bedside, beside this man to whom I was indifferent if not covertly hostile. As I looked into his face, I thought, *My God, he is going to die, and I'm not ready.* My life flashed before my eyes, and then I realized, *I am his son.* I saw my own impending death in his. I even saw the close resemblance in our physical features. My family as I had known it was soon to be broken, and it seemed I would be alone. Outside it was bitterly cold. Christmas was not the same for the next few years. This was like *my* "death" too and it was very different from the first two near-deaths. I was now a middle-aged man, and what I seemed to be missing gnawed at me more urgently than ever. My grief work began at this point, and it wasn't just for my father, but for my marriage of fifteen years, which was failing.

The winter of 1978 was my darkest and most difficult. I hit bottom. The phrase "midlife crisis" doesn't adequately cover it. Both during that winter and for some years after, I went to several counselors, all of whom were of some assistance to me even though I now see I was looking for an easy way out—out of entanglement in my marriage and the need to stand on my own two feet and give up control where things were beyond my control.[3]

It was mainly my father's death and my wife's increasing independence that allowed me to see how deeply dissatisfied I was with my life, and how empty I felt, an enigma in the midst of what I thought was success. And yet I was scared to do much about it. It wasn't until I found myself in front of a little Buddha-looking man named Phil in Riverside, California, in his counseling office, that the hole in my heart and the frequent ache in my solar plexus were fully acknowledged. Here was a man whom I had never met before and who knew nothing about me. Yet he seemed to know me instantly. Before I could say anything he looked at me with the dearest admiration and said, "God, Clint, you've been doing good, hard work." By this time (spring of 1983), because I saw the end of my twenty-four-year marriage in sight, I was crying a lot, which was new to me.

Phil spoke to the healing power of the process as if blame, shame, and the "let me try to fix it one more time" plea were suspended. He was definitely a male-mother to me. I didn't want to admit that I was saying goodbye to my marriage. In his tough, gentle Jungian language he 1) pointed out that I could not get from my wife what I was looking for, the deep feminine—because I already have it; 2) declared that my wife had saved me three trips to Tibet (where people go to get enlightened) because she had decided to leave me; and 3) urged me to get a gravestone marked "(my) marriage" and dance upon it. (Why did I have to come to see *this* crazy guy?) He spoke of the sleepwalking of many men and the need for their initiation with other men. He was the first to refer me to the writings of Robert Bly.

The divorce that followed in five months was quite amicable—I was thorough and sincere in making my amends to her, and we are now good friends—but the process of coming out into the world as a single man was new and difficult. It seemed like my deep social connection to life and others depended on my wife, and now she was gone. I often felt as though I had done something bad or, worse, that I *was* bad.

Later, I chose a mission that would pull myself back into life. As an expression of my stand for the sustainable end of world hunger by A.D. 2000, I ran the 10 K in the International Peace Marathon in Moscow in August of 1987, paying my own expenses. When our plane stopped in Iceland, I said to myself that I was now a citizen of the world. I'm grateful to my world runner friends for all their support. Inviting people and businesses to contribute financially to the mission (beyond my own expenses)—some four hundred of them—was a growth experience. Often I didn't want to do it.

Around this timer, 1987, I began to keep a daily journal, record all my dreams, write some poetry, go to some twelve-step meetings, and more consciously seek company with other men. And so I heard about The New Warrior Training Adventure for men, which three fellows from Milwaukee had created. It promised honor to men without being antifeminist. Most of all, it offered initiation and discovery of the Wild Man (see Chapter 8), gifts only men can give to other men. Male support groups were unknown to me up to this time. I remembered what Phil had said nearly seven years earlier. I was very hungry for this training. Men, such as I, were beating the door down to get in. I was "up on the diving board," and I jumped. The water was fine, yet the challenges I faced in that weekend were almost more than I could handle. Life with women doesn't necessarily get better for men after experiences such as the new warrior training, but it does get clearer because one has shifted how one sees oneself. Men have a chance to hear each other deeply and look at our shadows (see Chapter 8). Often passion, compassion, and mission arise for each participant's life. It's a chance for new beginnings.[4]

Some remarkable healing with my mother has recently occurred. Throughout my adult married life, my strain with her had continued. Usually, I did not want to be around her—maybe I saw too much of myself in her. I got the message from her to be a nice boy and successful. She also, I thought, hung on to me and, of course, I resisted. Phil had predicted there would be a change in my relationship with her if I took the initiative toward divorce, and he made some Zenlike comment that only when "a rope is cut clean does it cease to unravel," an aphorism I did not understand at the time. My mother worried about me throughout the divorce. I even remember, at age forty-nine, protesting to her that "It's time you treated me like a man." Her response surprised me: "I have, but you didn't get it."

Recently, in the summer, I planned early to go see her and told her, in effect, that she would have my undivided time. What happened was nothing short of a miracle. In the past when she had insisted on cooking for me, doing my laundry, or buying me a new shirt, I would get very irritated. This time I accepted all with gratitude. To top it off, we rented a car and together set off on a four-day, 950-mile journey into four little towns in North Dakota where we or she had lived or often visited in the past. We reminisced and laughed. Entanglement had dissolved and I cannot fully explain it. We were no longer codependent. When she and I looked in the mirror, I could now see both her *and me*.

As to my father? I now say that he did the best he could. Who am I to judge? I do know that my healing recently took a big step when I fully acknowledged that *I was* the little boy he whipped. At the time and afterward, because of the pain, it was as though I pictured "someone else" taking the beating. It was I. I was also extremely afraid of his rage, and later, angry. He shamed me, and I shamed him too. Now I see the anger is *mine*, and we'll talk more about anger later (Chapter 9) in this book.

In conclusion, I'd say that I have spent some time on my father and mother for a purpose. Michael Meade[5] suggests that the father gives us a curse (to the son it is a message something like "you're no good," "I'm busy," or "take care of *yourself*,"—see next chapter) and the mother gives us a spell due to the warmth of the amniotic fluid of the womb in which we are bathed during her pregnancy. (This message is more subtle—it shows up more like what I call sleepwalking.) These are the men's houses in which we move into life. These seem like harsh realities to us. There may be exceptions. Where the child is separated early from both the biological father and mother, there may still be the same outcome if father and mother surrogates carry the general culture of the society. The child is still helpless and dependent.

But what can we do, we ask? A simply answer may be cheating our own process, but it seems that recovery is marked first by looking at what our relationship to mother and father really was in our experience, by acknowledging that some kind of curse and spell may have happened, and by seeing that these wounds can be the source of power in people's lives if they're properly healed, though this is really never finished. This healing process often requires teaching, emotion work, communication, and initiation guided by elders or mentors. The latter part of this book is largely about that process.

EVALUATION

What I see is that I am not the only subject matter of this autobiography. Nor are my accomplishments the focus. I've taken and received richly from the collective of humankind both living and dead. I also see two kinds of journeys: One horizontal (the break from smaller to larger circles as I left the farm, went to college, to the marathon in Moscow) and one vertical (for example, lessons to be learned from my early tie with my mother, the death of my father, the breakdown of my marriage). These are like journeys within the journey and often involve crises that can stop us dead in our tracks.

I have attempted to write this autobiography[6] in the spirit of the sharing we encourage in men's groups as discussed in Chapter 9. Obviously some discretion is needed here in writing for a book for a general readership.

Autobiographies cannot claim respresentativeness of some larger sample of people. It is, therefore, appropriate to note a few differences and similarities: 1) Most men have not grown up in backward rural areas, in conservative religious communities, and they do not have graduate degrees as I do. 2) Most men who have siblings have at least one sister. Many men are not Caucasian. Most, probably, will not define their life crises as I did nor react to them as I did. In other ways, I may be quite similar to other men: a) Most of us as boys have experienced corporal punishment—some very severely. b) Probably most of us feel the pressure to accomplish more or to do better materially. c) Most of us have an emotional or competitive distance between ourselves and other men, starting with our fathers. d) Many of us fear violence and have difficulty grieving losses or feeling fully alive. We have often given up on our dreams and not seen the possibility of missions (see Chapter 9).

Since satisfaction, or the lack of it, appears to be a theme in much of human life, I shall now offer my definition, which is one up to which I have been working: Satisfaction is in some sense of assurance that, regardless of what occurs, one is held in esteem by some context of caring and safety in ourselves or with others or in a higher power.

In conclusion I also offer the following poem, "Red to White," which I wrote in honor of my fifty-eighth birthday.

Red to White

And now I am growing older.
In the colors of the four directions of the Sioux,
     north is red and south is white, and,
     it is said, a road connects them.
We begin to walk that road from the day we are born,
     from the north to the south.
When we are young and robust, we are red, and,
     as the years pass, walking that road,
     we become more white, our hair and skin.
At the end of the road in the south
     when we die, we rise into spiritland.

The physical body presents an enigma.
As our clay temple, it deserves
     the best care we can give it.
On the other hand, it is but a temporary dwelling
     and if we become highly attached to it,
     we shall be disappointed.
There is little conversation of this in our culture
     and so it must be said here.

NOTES AND REFERENCES

1. The title of an Irish ballad is: "Johnny, I Hardly Knew Ye." Johnny, at a young age, was killed in war.

2. The literature on men's friendships is complex and suffers, in my opinion, from the overfocus on the notion that men, with other men, are not self-disclosing. In regard to the reference here to my felt isolation, it appears that this is more common among upwardly mobile men. See Peter M. Nardi, ed., *Men's Friendships* (Newbury Park, Calif.: Sage Publications, 1992).

3. A distinction between attempting to control another and making (reasonable) requests should be made. Frequently, I made requests for love or favors of another that were really demands—she, for example, my wife, (I believed) had no option to decline; I *expected* the results (and in a particular shape or form). Obviously, I was often angry or disappointed—tired, too, because attempting that kind of control is *hard* work. On the other hand, request-making can enliven a relationship. Social psychologists point to

studies that indicate we can strengthen a relationship with another this way; we *like* to do things for others especially when that person is important to us, when we do them voluntarily, and when the other acknowledges us for their completion whatever the results look like. Request-making can also indicate trust and a willingness not to try to do everything ourselves. Making requests of another to change a behavior that bothers or scares us may also succeed if, in making it, we do not indict the *character* of the other.

4. Joseph Campbell's term, "following your bliss," comes to mind here. See his *The Hero with a Thousand Faces* (Princeton, N.J.: Princeton University Press, 1949).

5. *Men and the Water of Life: Initiation and the Tempering of Men* (San Francisco: Harper, 1993). I have, since The New Warrior Training Adventure, participated in other organized men's work such as mythopoetic-sponsored retreats and I have been in several men's support groups (see Chapter 9).

6. On the writing of biography see Louis M. Smith, "Biographical Method," in Norman K. Denzin and Yvonna S. Lincoln, eds., *Handbook of Qualitative Research* (Thousand Oaks, Calif.: Sage Publications, 1994), 286–301.

Chapter 4

Beginning in Life and the Boy in the Man

There is undoubtedly a wide gap for most of us between the "Congratulations-on-your-new-arrival" greeting cards we receive and the actual realities—for both parents and child. It's said that even the push out through the birth canal requires withstanding enormous pounds of traumatic pressure on the infant's head. Things don't get much better after that either.

The child is helpless and dependent. The primary care-giver, usually mother, comes and goes. She cannot hold the infant all the time. Maybe she doesn't even always know what the baby's needs are. What was it like when we as infants first urgently called out for help and no one responded? What was it like when she put us down and left? Would she ever return? For some of us, perhaps most, that was the first moment of fear of abandonment or fear that we were not loved. And, as John Bradshaw[1] asserts, sooner or later we're told to hold back or deny our feelings and to be quiet like good kids.

Most of us want to believe that when we become adults, we put away childish things. Yet it isn't true. The mark of the child is very much impressed upon the life of the adult. According to Lillian Rubin,[2] separation from mother is especially challenging for both sons and daughters. It is an ambivalent process: we need her, yet we begin to want some autonomy as well. Osherson says it well: (Due to the structure of the family) "early on we experience women as the ones who fill us up, who comfort and take care of us without having an opportunity in growing up to learn how to fill ourselves and to feel full while truly separate from women."3 Mother, or mother substitutes, are powerful. They give and take away. Once we can crawl, we go out (away from her) and come back, over and over, as we test the field of range. Generally she gives comfort when we come back after going out and "getting burned." (Maybe we bumped into something sharp or hot or got lost or whatever.)

The situation for the son has its own special complications. Since both attachment and incipient identity with the mother occur early and together, some processes are set in motion for girls and boys that are fundamentally different, according to Rubin: the boy is born of woman (as is the daughter), yet he is a male (which the daughter is not). In some ways he does not belong. Identifying who he is is problematical. There may be some subtle erotic attachment between mother and son as well. He (the son) must separate more quickly and sharply than his sister does—even renounce her who has been a vital part of himself. He may be left in a very vulnerable (unprotected) position. The shift in identification away from mother will be painful for the son, and he may at the same time begin to distrust her support, his attachment, and even show some contempt for that which represents woman or the feminine. His inner world has gone through a huge upheaval.

He suffers a wound of loss, and it is not fully expressible later because some of it comes at an early, preverbal period of infancy. Yet the pain is there even if suppressed. On top of a shaky gender identity he will fashion tight and rigid defenses against an uncertain world: I'd better look out for just myself. Challenges to manage or negotiate interpersonal relations with strong emotional undertones will likely be difficult throughout life.

As we let go of mother, somehow and to some degree, the script says that sons identify with father. Osherson examined this process, looking back in the lives of 370 men now in their forties who graduated from Harvard in the 1960s. The news is not good. Most did not find their fathers, did not connect: in fact, "Boys grow into men with a wounded father within, a conflicted inner sense of masculinity rooted in men's experience of their fathers as rejecting, incompetent or absent."[4] Father was experienced by these sons as judgmental and angry or, in other cases, as needy or vulnerable. He might have seemed entrapped in his duties from day to day, empty of life-giving passion or purpose, and, above all, remote. Often, sons found it much more fun to be around mom in the domestic world of coziness, play, and understanding.

Fathers might be protectors and providers, but they weren't experienced as nurturers in the interpersonal sense; either they hadn't learned how to nurture, or they were not around or available to do it.

But there may be another reason, and this is more the heart of the matter for Osherson: Nurturing is impeded by the wounds that men do not talk about, *viz.*, their darkest fears, inadequacies, insecurities, weaknesses—even their sense of helplessness, worthlessness, and neediness. To do so (to talk) clashes with success images for men and might bring up feelings of anger or sorrow that simply have too much charge on them.[5] So we hide them or stuff them in a black box and go on pretending not to see what we all see or sense. Sons don't talk about this with fathers because fathers didn't talk about this with their fathers, and so on. Lineally it is a multicompounded wound, perhaps more than two thousand years old. As Bly says, "we limp our father's limp." We secretly bear his and our shame.[6] When major troubles arise—loss of money, failures at work, the birth of a child, the first child leaving home, the death of a loved one, an unwanted divorce— we stumble through or tough it out. Few of us are willing or know how to emotionally hold a man in severe upset. It's a risk because he is disturbed by both the immediate crisis *and* all that it triggers from childhood—his unfinished business with mother or father.

I can relate to this. One time I sat in my car all alone in a parking lot after a series of very trying episodes in a relationship. It was one of those dreary days in the spring—heavy clouds in the sky and a raw breeze that seemed to go through me. I tried to ascertain my feelings and I then took some notes for my journal. I wanted to catch myself on the spot because I'd felt like that before, and always, when it passed, it didn't seem real anymore, and I forgot it or couldn't recreate its power close enough to the raw experience.

As I look back on those notes now, I see the multilayered pain and confusion Osherson often found in the men he interviewed. One level was the upset itself and the blame and insecurity that often went with it. On deeper levels I felt defective, shamed, and unloved. My attempts to be loved were sometimes blunted by my own neediness.[7] The feeling is really one of deep sorrow, accompanied by thoughts to the effect that I'm no good. I noticed and wrote about bodily sensations, especially a tightness in my throat and a hollow in my solar plexus. Some anger accompanied my sense of powerlessness (Can't I control things? I can't do anything about her withdrawal from me. Maybe I deserved it anyway.) Sometimes, as in this case, I feared *I* was disintegrating at the core, that I couldn't hold myself together, that I might not have the will or resources to go on to concentrate and do my everyday jobs. Above all, I felt alone.

That was ten years ago. I had barely gotten in touch with the normality of those feelings for men, nor in touch with men I could call on the telephone, who could hear me. Since then, I have felt those same feelings, though not often. Today I can call a trusted friend who is likely to say, I hear you, my brother, and I want you to know you are no less of a man for feeling and sharing this. Sometimes he will "speak me back to myself": You are lonely, you are very sad, you shake in your boots. We don't analyze it all. There is a wonderful power in simply *listening* and acknowledging what's going on. And I have done this for my friend too.

Why are we talking about this now, now in the 1990s? In large part because such suffering has always been there and in large part too because the times have changed. Social changes, such as the larger numbers of women entering paid employment and the fragility of marriages have created a great upheaval. "Earth mother," the woman who pretended to need our protection and in turn took care of us, "is dead," declared Herb Goldberg in his 1976 book.[8] Traditional guidelines floundered. A new scorecard seemed to emerge in the 1960s as various women's-rights groups spoke out loudly about men's presumed defects, irresponsibility, or insensitive dominance. Many men found their lives thrown into confusion and disrespect.

Jed Diamond[9], in an insightful biography, tells of the struggles in his marriage and in other intimate relations with women: his desire to be loved and recognized; the tie of his feelings to hers; his conflict when she wanted him to be strong (even stick up for himself), and he needed to be softer; and his feeling of fear she'd leave. He also felt guilt when she showed her independence and he became threatened, but didn't think he was entitled to his fear (after all no one should impede the quest of another for her happiness). He wrote of feeling alone, his difficulty in deciding what he needed and then asking for it. So he found himself flip-flopping (How can you hold your poise while tied to someone you so desperately need?) every two or three weeks in relationship crises, hoping, later, life would get better. There is a cycle of entanglement here: anger or disappointment, followed by attempts to get back at the other or withdraw love or take some remedial action (even to gain some small amount of healthy detachment) followed by apology, again, when someone's feelings are hurt. She's up and he's down, then, later, it might be the other way around.[10] Knots like these in cross-gender unions are probably very common, according to Rubin—and only a very few couples have the will or resources to dissolve them by themselves.

It is not likely to be easy to process the black box stuff in the presence of women, especially those with whom we're intimate. Most frequently they expect men to be grown up already. How can he fight with me or become pitifully helpless and then want to make love? she asks. Of course she gets hurt, too, in many of these confrontations. Many men will at least initially feel safer processing these issues among other men who are also willing to honestly share them in a protected and affirming group and to change.

Over the years I've taught a junior-level course for college students titled Sex and Gender in Society. We tend to limit each section to forty-five students and, even when we offer several sections, many students who want to get into the course cannot. Usually the ratio of women to men in the class is around three or four to one, and, semester after semester, the men hardly ever speak up. Women do most of the talking and I generally enjoy that. One day, though, I came to class and opened up with the blunt question: "Why don't the men talk in here?" Silence. Finally, a man said, "Because I'm afraid I'll get clobbered by the women if I do." Do you know what happened? He did get clobbered by the women as they groaned in disgust in response to his comment, suggesting he was too thin skinned.

As I said in my own story, around the time of my divorce I began to cry. At first it was like manipulative crying in hopes that it would get my wife's attention and cause her to yield in my direction. I was in crisis and the crying was sometimes quite uncomfortable or embarrassing. Sometimes, though, I seemed to be crying the deep sadness of many generations. Later, the crying came more out of genuine grief for the loss I was experiencing and anticipating.

Like a good sociologist, I decided to do a study of crying among college students. I noticed that very little had been written about the topic, especially regarding men. I took a nonrandom sample: approximately 185 students in four general university classes that drew a broad cross section of men and women mainly in the eighteen to twenty-two-year-old bracket.[11] I administered an anonymous questionnaire and balanced the respondents into a group of eighty-six women and eighty-six men for comparison. I wanted to find out the how, where, and with whom of crying. I also wanted to know about the intensity and frequency. I asked about times when the students might have been present when someone else cried as well as times when they themselves cried and who else was present.

The findings were quite dramatic. Eighty percent reported that in the last two years they had seen (been in the actual presence of) at least one man who cried, and 97 percent had seen at least one woman cry. Eighty percent of the men and 100 percent of the women students admitted they had cried in the last two years, but only 10 percent of the men had cried nine times or more, whereas 73 percent of the women had. Also, it appeared that men felt less well about themselves afterward and probably tended to cry at a lower intensity. They also cried in front of a woman more often than in front of a man and for shorter durations when with a man. Most surprising, an equal percentage of men and women said they would like to be able to cry more often when crying was needed. Generally, we can say that the study indicated that crying by men was much less frequent than by women and that it was not as supported or productive, especially when men cried in the presence of other men.

That study was in 1980 and is probably still true of most college men today in that age bracket. Seven years later I did The New Warrior training weekend mentioned in my autobiography. Here crying broke out several times, which countered what I found in 1980. Of course the training drew a more selective population. Here, crying was much more supported and encouraged healing among the men. Once, during an especially powerful exercise, a father (who had been working there that weekend as a facilitator) ended up being held in the lap and arms of his seventeen-year-old son (a participant). Both were crying profusely. I was moved very, very deeply. I looked around the room among the nearly forty other men there; there wasn't a dry eye anywhere. I sat there crying, too, from the bottom of my guts, and today, seven years later, I recall those old men weeping deeply as they prayed aloud in German in the little church I attended as a kid. Could they have kept the seeds of crying alive for all of us?

Recently I went to a for-men-only talk, sponsored by our local community hospital on men and loss/grieving. When the psycho-therapist finished his presentation, he asked, "What else would you like?" Silence. I looked around at the some twelve or thirteen men in attendance. I noticed at least eight who appeared to be over sixty-five. One of them slowly raised his hand and said, "I'd like to know who's here." We then started with our self-introductions. When his turn came, he pursed his lips tightly, fighting back the tears. He shared that his wife of fifty-six years had just died (in this hospital) three weeks ago and, now as the tears broke loose, he managed to push out a voice that said, "And I miss her something terrible." Soon, he discovered that at least six other men present were in the same situation.

What I saw was that they had put almost all their eggs in the proverbial basket, and now the basket was empty (she was gone—one said he had no offspring, only his little dog), that they were very isolated, and that they were in pain. By the time the evening was over, most of them had reached out a little to each other and/or had some plans to join a bereavement group sponsored by the local hospice organization. But these men were the exception. They were probably only the few. They were present. Where do the other men whose wives die first go? What do they do? Do they suffer in silence and go to their death soon after their wife has died?[12]

Osherson has done some marvelous pioneering work with men. He dares to ask the questions that open up the black box and he listens empathetically as men move into their many discomfort zones. Osherson is fair; he lets us know where men need to be both understood and more understanding. He honors the courage of the men he has talked to and their resiliency. He seems flexible and accepting: sometimes men want to take only a small step or have only a short word of healing with their fathers, while others go much deeper. Sometimes our fathers are already dead or they might snub any attempts we might make at healing in which case we will have to do what we can without them. I myself remembered the incident of my father standing tall against the bitter winter winds, driving my brother and me to school in the horse-drawn, open sled a few months after he died.

Osherson offers us insights for how we can find men's desire for connectivity showing up in their back-handed jokes or pranks, their aggressiveness, their hard work, or their stoic self-protectiveness. He adds a myriad of glimpses into his own fears as he enters and leads men's workshops and into the falterings and successes of being a son, father, and husband himself, something which makes him as a therapist much more human.

There is, however, more I'd like to add to his good work: this involves both more in the sense of reaching out to poorer men (his were Harvard graduates) and more in the sense of utilizing imaginal and spiritual power. Later (Chapter 9), I will mention my experience and work with men in twelve-step programs that reach millions of men (and women) and cost almost no money. While I see no panacea in twelve-step work (and I'm aware of some of the intellectual criticisms against it), it dares to invoke that which is unseen.

I have noticed that when women started their transformative efforts in the 1960s they had no trouble invoking the Goddess Within, exclaiming their *value* positions even in academic/scientific textbooks (I'm a feminist!), creating both consciousness-raising and power-reclaiming groups for self-respect *and* action, stating their conditions without apology for becoming their own person (woman). This is some of the gold I'd like to add to Osherson's good work in future chapters of this book.

I have a hunch that men pick up some of their tenderness by imitating women who display tenderness, but this is not completely authentic; a man's real tenderness will come through the discovery of his own deeper masculinity, and that is likely to emerge only when he goes through his own root crisis[13] often in the company of other men; then both fierceness and tenderness will be available. More on this in future chapters.

At this point, we can say that our journey is likely to include confrontation with the black box stuff, the boy within the man, as well as the growth that comes from wrestling with, and hopefully out of, our unhealthy entanglements. The journey usually takes us down into our shame, the shakiness of our powerlessness and our sadness.

EVALUATION

The separation of son from mother topic raises some methodological issues, one of the largest of which is the fact that some of it begins before the child has much ability to verbalize. Therefore, the researcher cannot be sure what the boys' actual experiences were. Also, these researchers may carry the bias that the early years are the most fundamental in personality formation. Obviously, learning and change goes on throughout life and produces, in different situations, more diversity in the lives of both girls and boys than I have discussed here. On a more political note there may be the *appearance* that the mother (or mother surrogate) is being blamed for any negative outcomes. Finally, there is the difference in perspective between structuralists (mentioned earlier at the end of Chapter 1) who see role-cues and rewards from institutional arrangements of the society more determinative of conduct than earlier learned psycho-social dynamics in the small family group.[14]

The research on men's relationship with their fathers reported in this chapter focuses on a midlife view looking back. That is (in Osherson's study) these were Harvard men mostly in their forties looking back at their (now) aging fathers. What of children and their fathers today? It seems mostly fathers are still absent or unresponsive most of the time, even when no divorce has occurred. It is not easy to assess the impact of father absence or distance alone on the son since other factors such as the reason for the absence or the mother's attitude in regard to his absence play a role too. In some important studies recently, however, there seems to be some growing evidence for the conclusion that the quality of mental health of the son is more dependent on his relationship to his father than to his mother.[15]

It takes little observation in this society to notice the father deficit, yet there is little institutional support for fathering and father training. Very little discussion exists on the topic even in marriage and family textbooks except to say: 1) that fathers go through some distress when their wives give birth, face a new sense of high responsibility, and sometimes feel left out when the mother and infant are closely united; 2) that fathers sex-type children more than mothers, treating male and female children differently (such as in handling, games, or toys); and 3) almost as an afterthought, that given the opportunity, time, and encouragement "fathers are or can be just as nurturant as mothers."[16] More on this chapter in Chapter 6.

For several years now I have been gathering family background reports from my students at the beginning of each semester. I began to notice a rather large number of students who voluntarily eluded to the high respect they had for their fathers. Some of them reported that their fathers had actually held down two or three jobs early in the marriage so that the family (including two or three children) could survive. Some fathers continued to do so now that the child was in college. This seemed like a fugitive fact to me—one overlooked because of a general neglect of fathers in our culture. I decided to pursue the question of fathers more systematically with a short questionnaire answered in two introductory Sociology classes. Students in these sections came from a broad range of majors (business, fine arts, sciences) in the university.

The results from twenty-eight females and twenty-eight males, mostly nineteen and twenty year olds, surprised me: 1) To the statement, "I admire the efforts my father makes to the survival and maintenance of our family," all students moderately or highly agreed, except two men and one woman. Highly agree answers outnumbered moderately agree by two to one.[17] 2) When asked to pick adjectives (positive or negative) out of a list that the student said best fits his/her father or mother, the following results were obtained: mothers were described as loving by forty-one students (equally split between male and female respondents), supportive/helpful by thirty-eight students (by slightly more males), and reliable by twenty-nine students (by slightly more males again); fathers were described as reliable by thirty-five students (by slightly more males) and supportive/helpful by thirty-four students (by slightly more males), and loving by twenty-three students (by more females). Also, fathers were described as humorous by twenty students (by slightly more males), and closed minded by seventeen students (almost equally by males and females). Finally, mothers were described as good listeners by a vote of twenty-three to three over fathers. Again, the latter might imply that fathers aren't around (available) as much as mothers to be good listeners.

The point to all of this, however, is that this was a blind spot to me. I did not previously see the rather positive way fathers were regarded.

NOTES AND REFERENCES

1. John Bradshaw, *Bradshaw on the Family* (Deerfield Beach, Fla.: Health Communications, Inc., 1988).

2. Lillian Rubin, *Intimate Strangers* (New York: Harper & Row, 1983).

3. Samuel Osherson, *Finding Our Fathers* (New York: The Free Press, 1986), 7.

4. Osherson, 4.

5. Also, see Samuel Osherson, *Wrestling With Love* (New York: Fawcett Columbine, 1992).

6. The idea or feeling that one is defective or bad at the core of one's being. Shame messages tend to make an air-tight case *against* ourselves.

7. One of the ways this happens is neatly illustrated in the following self-made trap—He: "Do you love me?" She: "Yes, I love you." He: "Do you *really* love me?" She (almost irritated now): "Yes." And so it goes on. Looking for certainty in this area, or demanding it, can be self-defeating.

8. Herb Goldberg, *The Hazards of Being Male* (New York: Nash Publishing, 1976).

9. Jed Diamond, *Inside Out: Becoming My Own Man* (San Raphael, Calif.: Fifth Wave Press, 1983).

10. This would appear to follow the pattern of codependency in addictive relations, where one or both longs for the other (intimate partner) when s/he is absent, but, also, where one finds that being with her/him doesn't make things better either (like an alcoholic wanting a drink, but finding that, when s/he takes it, its aftermath doesn't make things better). What happens here for example, in a dyadic close relationship is that *both partners* are tied too much to the other. There are usually three roles present: perpetrator, victim, and rescuer. When she's down, he can feel strong, and even gain some halo by caretaking her (rescuing) from the perpetrator (whatever or whoever forced her down). When he's down (a victim), he may blame her (or whomever), demand her broad attention, or expect a quick cure. Much of this pattern is anchored in a deep insecurity or sense of being unlovable. Here is where a men's (or women's) group can be of great value: 1) in getting a sense of the source of the codependency, the ability, in some matters, to take care of oneself, and the ways of managing feelings and preventing the destructive acting out from them that might arise, as well as 2) in receiving acknowledgment and spiritual reassurance from other members of the group regarding one's value as a human being.

11. Clinton Joyce Jesser, "Men and Crying," *Changing Men* 12, (Winter/Spring, 1989), 72–73. Also see Carol Staudacher, *Men & Grief* (Oakland, Calif.: New Harbinger Publications, Inc., 1991).

12. The literature on widows is rather extensive; on widowers it is rather skimpy. See Robert C. Atchley, *Social Forces and Aging* (Belmont, Calif.: Wadsworth, 1994), 164–166 and 354–356. For a concurring note regarding men's isolation, see Jenny De Jong-Gierveld, "Husbands, Lovers, and Loneliness," in Robert A. Lewis and Robert E. Salt, eds., *Men in Families* (Beverly Hills, Calif.: Sage Publications, 1986), 115–125. Also, see Edward H. Thompson, Jr., ed., *Older Men's Lives* (Thousand Oaks, Calif.: Sage Publications, 1994).

13. This may involve the question of his own identity and what it is to be a man.

14. See, for example, Joseph Pleck, *The Myth of Masculinity* (Cambridge, Mass.: MIT Press, 1981). The view that I have presented here, however, departs considerably from the Male Sex Role Identity Paradigm, which he critiques. There is a debate among academicians/advocates on the

issue of splitting. Some (largely) feminists say that fathers gender-type (split/separate) boys (sons) from girls (daughters) more than mothers do, and that this is not good (in a context of androgyny). It is, therefore, better to push fathers out (exclude them) and let the boy retain the feminine virtues of the mother. For a summary of some of this view, and a differing opinion, see David Blankenhorn, *Fatherless America* (New York: Basic Books, 1995), 90–93.

15. See Christopher T. Kilmartin, *The Masculine Self* (New York: Macmillan, 1994), 264.

16. See Mary Ann Schwartz and Barbara Marline Scott, *Marriages and Families* (Englewood Cliffs, N.J.: Prentice-Hall, 1994), 287. Also, see David Popenoe's view that it is an error to try to make fathers more like mothers. He asserts that positive fathering has its own contribution to make. See *Society* 30 (September/October, 1993), 5–11.

17. The seven cases of fathers permanently absent were omitted.

Chapter 5

Sex, Sex-Craving, and Relationships

It's easy to think that our sexual desires and identities come full blown into our lives without any personal or societal history. That's not true, of course. Sexualities are constructed in society, and that society has a history. Church, family, and economics are all involved. In the West, early Christian church leaders (fathers) created a false dichotomy between body and spirit, elevating the latter to Godliness. Their attempts to practice celibacy probably contributed to seeing women either as pure beings (above it all, like Mary) or as temptresses. Men were, on the other hand, seen as tough and carnal.

Later, in the fifteenth and sixteenth centuries, with the emergence of courtly and then romantic love, the notions of sex and caring became intertwined. As the new middle classes emerged with their ideal separation of the husband's and the wife's spheres (public and private respectively), the arrangement required that husbands provide sexual fidelity and economic support in exchange for the wife's domestic labor, (legitimate) children, and purity (including her emotional work and support). Beginning with the emergence of the romantic novel in the fourteenth century, it was largely women who defined the standards for love, feeling, and intimate relationships.[1] Much of this ethic is still with us today.

Researchers have studied various facets of sexuality: Kinsey[2] tried to take an across-the-board survey. In his pioneering studies in the

1940s, he asked about the frequency of premarital and extramarital sex as well as such things as homosexuality and masturbation. Much research of this type sought to measure the gap between the Victorian norms espoused by many and actual behavior. Masters and Johnson[3] pioneered in another direction: they studied how to help people (couples) who were seeking to overcome certain dysfunctions such as premature ejaculation, impotence, low sexual desire, and orgasmic absence.

When the topic is sex, almost no one is believed to be value neutral, not even scientists. We all are accused of having our axe to grind, our prejudices and fears. It's a contentious and uneasy topic. Lately, the rancor over sex has heated up both from the feminist left—who have condemned male sexual abuse and addiction, pornography, inappropriate male aggression, and inequality in the bedroom as reflective of inequality in society at large—and from the moral right, who usually defend a sex-in-marriage-only standard and decry homosexuality. In the middle is the newly emerged fear and controversy over AIDS and other sexually transmitted diseases.

When I ask my female students to anonymously write down what it is men don't understand about sex, several themes emerge: that they (women) often want (need) intimacy, affection, and closeness from men before, during, and after sex; that sex and seriousness or commitment must go together; and that because of other concerns or multiple responsibilities, a woman cannot always be expected to be ready for sex whenever the man is. My male students, on the other hand, list quite different themes in response to the question of what it is women don't understand about sex: that it's o.k. sometimes to separate love and sex; that men have a strong sex drive and need sex often; that a man can be aroused easily; and a few say that men need to be hugged and caressed too—that *they* want to feel wanted, not just be seen as only wanting sex.

Most of these students are quite young (eighteen to twenty-two), and obviously more dialogue is needed between these men and women. Most of them have socialized to a large extent in gender-segregated groups from age eight to ten on —the boys here, the girls there. They have come to treat each other with some suspicion—neither wants to be taken advantage of. The circumstances that allow the possibility for consensual sex between two adults who communicate their needs, compromise, and enhance mutual pleasure are lacking. What's quite clear here is that the men expect to be quite "hungry" and to pursue sex. Farrell even asserts that part of men's put-down of women derives from the face-saving they must salvage in anticipation of, or in response to, women's rejections.[4] Men don't get a chance to say no because women seldom ask or initiate in a way men notice or understand. I shall now switch to a particular scene, the strip or go-go show, from which I want to discuss the phenomenon of what I call "male sexual hunger," but first I begin with a poem I wrote.

UNFINISHED BUSINESS

Once the earth-people got together
    and they said, "Let's have sex"
The men said "Yah!" and the women said, "Oh, O.K."
So they did
    So they did
       So they did
Soon the men were saying: "We need it,"
    and the women were saying: "We've got it, but we'll
       give it to you only if we like, afterall:
          sometimes there is pregnancy, which we suffer—
          and immorality, which is when we say it is wrong—
          and STD'S, which we don't want—
          and our busy schedules—
          and it's dirty and often no fun—
          and, besides, men are jerks 'cuz they don't understand
          or respect us."
So, the problem was all those men who said
    they needed it (couldn't get enough)—
    and the price kept going up—
So, some men took it by force, and
   some bought it from women on the street, and
   some became brilliant suitors and
   some did it with other men, and
   some did without. Almost all of the men bought more *Playboys*
    and so did their sons—
Seems like the lines were drawn—nothing gave
Until some men started a men's group, and then—

I realize that in presenting the poem, I am on very subjective grounds—poems take some liberty with verified truth, and involve metaphors and intuitions. Even more, this is a poem written by me, and it might be said that it is largely a product of my issues and way of seeing. Some readers of the poem say, Yes, that's the way it is, or That's interesting. Others say, Too bad, men deserve their plight (see evaluation section), while still others say that, in their experience, the *women* have had the stronger libido. At any rate, what is clear is that we are talking about a condition of neediness (craving) in the face of unfinished business.

Sometimes when I was in a large city, I went, usually alone, to a show-girl club. These are businesses, usually on the edge of downtown or in tourist areas because of zoning regulations, and the windows are darkened or shaded. These are adult-only places, which usually charge an at-the-door admission. They may also require that the customer buy a minimum number of alcoholic drinks. Except for the female performers and waitresses, the customers are usually all males, some young (twenties), and some middle aged, dressed moderately well. Some are in groups and some alone.

Inside, the scene is focused on young, shapely, almost nude women "dancing" (in high heels) to music on a stage in spotlights. Often, a dancer will look down, meet eye-to-eye with a male spectator near the stage, and, by bolder suggestive bodily movements, signal her interest in receiving a money-tip from him. A sort of spell is cast. Verbal interchange with the men is low (the music is usually too loud anyway). Usually the customers are forbidden from even touching the dancers, unless it's a "lower-class" bar, in which case, legally or illegally, for more money, such contact might come later and in areas removed from the main show.

When I describe this scene to my students in the Sex and Gender class, I usually got several reactions. For one group of students (usually women) this type of business and what goes on there is absolutely morally wrong. Though I usually do not query them in detail as to why they object, it's quite obvious that certain conventional proprieties are violated here. The women are nude, or nearly so, and dancing for erotic purposes in front of men who are strangers. This does *not*

conform to the script most women learn in our society: *slow*-develop-
ing intimacy in exclusive-pair, cross-gender relationships in which
men take more of the initiative and women hint more subtly. Other
students object because they say it is exploitive of women.

A third group, the egalitarians, say it's wrong only if women are
forbidden from going to "their" shows where men are the performers.
A variation of this are those who say that men who have already-ex-
isting commitments of an intimate sort with a woman should not go.
Others (especially women) think it's not wrong—just weird; and still
others (especially men) say it's fine, why not?

Setting aside some of the moral objections temporarily, we can see
that the show-girl scene is fairly normal or reflective of themes in
everyday life for many men. It's an adventure. There is an opportunity
to satisfy some curiosity to see women's bodies. Some type of sexual
experience, often accompanied by fantasy, is available—eros without
responsibility. The exchange of money makes the scene patently
counterfeit, but men do get some kind of attention from women with
desirable looks and dimensions. The women are beautiful but unat-
tainable. The men "want"; the women hold back, even tease.

I'm sure men who go to these shows, where they are available, do
so for many different reasons. Some years later after sampling some of
these shows, I began asking myself these questions: Why am I drawn
to these women who fit a desirable image? (Is it a soft addiction, driven
out of a deeper underlying need or trauma that occurred earlier in my
life?) What is the chase doing to me? Why is it usually unsatisfying?

Several answers come to mind. One is the feminine does not equal
masculine in this society, nor do they even overlap much. Men, as well
as women, are then left with an apparent lack, an incompletion.
Feminine is good[5] in the sense of being identified with purity and
compassion[6] and, because we may think we have no feminine qualities, men must find them in a female, especially one who will enhance
our status or give us pleasure, and perhaps one who will help us identify
and process our emotional experience as well. Osherson's assertion (in
the previous chapter) that "early on we experience women as the ones
who fill us up . . . " seems appropriate. A key idea here holds that since
boys are of a different gender than their mother, when we separate

from her, there is less certainty of our gender identity, and therefore we are more susceptible to becoming pursuers of the female. This may make us seem hyper-masculine as well.

Also from a certain age (eight, ten, twelve?) on up, boys experience very little (gentle) touching, which is basic to emotional and interpersonal health. Resisting our need for it may cause us to crave it even more. Nor do boys and men receive and give themselves much nurturance—that delightful attention to ourselves beneath our facade, to the inner life that needs stroking from time to time. The need for touching and nurturance gets displaced as sexual cravings, and men may look to women for their satisfaction or even as just stimulus objects, especially when we are somewhat lonely or feeling "flat."

When men go to a strip show, they can go for the good time: visual (vicarious) enjoyment of anonymous women doing acts on stage generally forbidden in ordinary life. Or could they be looking for something deeper? Maybe, but take it for what it is.

Some distinction between excitement and passion may be helpful. Excitement is a craving and almost always the enemy of passion. Excitement usually responds to neediness. We grab at it in an attempt to fill a felt lack, or in an attempt to get a quick fix, to soothe a wound or prop up our spirits. Excitement doesn't request; it gets, takes, demands, but never satisfies. It thrives in artificiality and temporality like the strip show. One goes from one show to another for a new boost, or one tries in vain to find the situation that really fits one's ideal or needs as dictated by one's lonely or truculent inner child. This follows an addictive pattern and leads to disappointment and self-betrayal. Such excitement is a key to toxic sex. In other words, coming from excitement, one doesn't find something deeper and, maybe, one can't get what one *thinks* he wants or needs in *any* real situation or relationship with women.

Passion, on the other hand, is deeper and it comes from taking care of oneself, being responsible for one's feelings (including anger, loneliness, and sorrow), appreciating mundane life, mutuality, communicating honestly, apologizing when wrong, requesting reasonable help, and exposing oneself to healthy diversity. Passion honors both the good times and the hard times in a life. Passion often comes from surviving the ordeals of initiation.[7]

Sometimes sex leads to or follows from a relationship between the sexes. In the olden days, parents or kin took a hand in finding mates for men and women. Today all that's left are the referrals to eligible mates from family or friends. Sometimes we date people we already know as friends; sometimes we step into competitive markets of strangers to make direct contacts for ourselves or to make a deal as in singles bars and even classified advertisements. Caveat emptor. At any rate, when dating (or whatever it is called nowadays) begins to occur, we move from appreciating the outer appearance of another to sharing our inner lives—hopes, fears, quirks, gifts.

Listening to conversations, I find that most people don't seem well satisfied with intimate cross-gender relationships. Maybe we expect too much. After all, in the romantic ideal we are supposed to find the *one*, unexpectedly, and, as a result of some magical merger with him/her, live happily ever after if love is present. Bingo. Transformation. Or maybe romance is that temporary escape *from* an ongoing, committed relationship. My guess is that most men and women in love in new relationships, spending a lot of time together, will wear each other out in less than three weeks. Most people seem puzzled when a "hot" relationship turns cold and ends. Sometimes we make up some blame against the other to save face. In talking with my male students about this, I often see an attempt to match from the outside a feminine picture (glamorous woman) with something we thought we lacked inside us (I'm sure this is true for women too). There is a cultural stereotype (the *model* female) here, of course, but mystics go so far as to say we may be trying to merge the "over-soul" (for which we've substituted the woman) and the "inner-soul" (our own).

John Lee[8] makes it even more intelligible. He postulates a princess in all of us men—our own—and it is our duty (to our health) not to give her away, which is what we do when we see *that* (right) woman out there who immediately captures our fancy. Wow. A warrior spirit is helpful here: to say to myself, *Oh no, Clinton, she* (that woman) *looks gorgeous and bigger-than-* (mundane) *life, but you have a princess* (or a hole in your heart) *to take care of first.* Also, a "father thirst" may be involved. The (image of the) beautiful woman can sway us easily because we have no solid grounding for ourself. Our mature father is missing.[9]

Now for the poem's title, "Unfinished Business." What I've noticed is that most men in good men's work produce a shift in their intimate and committed relationships, which is often a joy to both partners. (See Chapters 8 and 9.) How is this possible? What is involved? What has happened?

First, in men's groups (see Chapter 9), men may begin to face their wounds, their sexual cravings, their fears and anger, in a safer place. They can hug each other too. They elicit feelings, name them, and feel them without judgment at their own pace. This is very important. By doing this, men need no longer be as defensive about them in dealings with women. Men can also get a new sense of what it is to be supported (respected) by other men in the group in a noncompetitive way, and even make some promises within the group to make amends to those they've harmed. Some men may choose to do a thorough inventory of themselves—both their positive and negative qualities—and share some of that with someone in the group in a setting of confidentiality. Women I've talked with deeply appreciate this. Men may also come to understand, realistically, that women have *their* agendas and vicissitudes too. One can also discover (often by feedback from others) what are our *own* issues in a relationship and what are *hers.*

Second is mission. Women often complain that when they ask men what they want, most say they don't know. Mission can be explored very effectively in men's groups as we shall see in Chapter 9. When mission is accompanied by commitment, goals, and projects, men may begin to find out what they want. Joy (JOY) is said to be a journey outside yourself, that is, an embracement of something large and life giving.

Third comes pride, heritage, and continuity. In men's groups, in sharing conversation, reading, and story telling, men have the privilege of getting in touch with a rich tradition of positive masculinity (see, for instance, the discussion of the archetypes in Chapter 8) to discover male modes of feeling, the struggles of our ancestors, and a closer connection to the earth and higher power. Especially important to sexuality here is pride in men's generativity. "Generative" in the dictionary says "having the power to produce or originate." A full appreciation of this is some solid ground for a man's self-esteem, and might enhance his relationship with women. In part, this is what's deeper. How about: "When I'm having an erection I'm standing on sacred ground (and I don't have to do anything about it)," or, "I now declare my gender ground as a whole man." (Say it aloud).

In closing, I'd like to speak of the possibility of "yielding" in intimate relationships. So much cynicism, sarcasm, and distrust deriving from the antipathy of the two cultures (men and women) exist in our society. So much of our folklore strongly admonishes each partner to a fifty-fifty relationship rather than a one hundred-one hundred. An endless number of books are written on improving fifty-fifty partnerships. The true warrior (see Chapter 8) is usually doing battle with *himself* first. He surrenders and looks inward, maybe at his own shortcomings. He learns to make choices and alter those if the consequences for him are undesirable. He must learn when a relationship is nonpassionate, to look at what *he* is not putting into it or into his life in general. Surrender and love go hand and hand. Gender war can start moving to gender peace and reconciliation for many of us.

Love is a willful act of caring deeply about and for the welfare of another. It also involves all the good work we do to take care of ourself so we remain, incidentally, attractive to another. Yielding is to give up our fight to be right. It allows us to deeply acknowledge the other, to play the man-woman game from the spirit of win/win—for her and for him. Obviously I'm not saying that a man (or a woman) should stay in a relationship where she or he is demeaned, abused, or exploited. No amount of surrender is appropriate here. What I am saying is more akin to the Buddhist version of karma: as I understand it, it holds that roughly what goes out (from us), comes back. What we reap, we've sown (though not always in the same *form*). From this standpoint when we take ourselves as good, loving, forgiving people and act on these convictions, we powerfully enhance our relationships.

69

his chapter, we can say that sex and sexuality are
. Sexual hunger is a driving force. We might keep
tions that do not exist. Or it might drive us to where
tive to take a look—into ourselves. This journey
us to where there is some hope of healing—to
supportive connections with other men.

EVALUATION

Sex and sexuality are multifaceted topics—for example, physiological, psychological, sociological and moral. When we add a cross-cultural point of view, we see even more variation and complexity in the matter. It has been noted that, in our society, there has been both a denial of sex and a sort of titillation with it (especially in advertisements). Indeed, one can see the latter as a derivative of the former when we open the door only half way in our public and private dialogues.

Sex is, of course, the root of reproduction based on fertility, but when reproduction is no longer an imperative for the society, its communicative aspects (for example, sex as a sign of love) and its significance in generalizing energy to other behaviors (for example, an expressive necktie or a sexy walk) emerge. Today, we are even talking about safe cyber-sex where the virtual reality of sex is available on the telephone, the computer internet, or in simulated play space with two or more people.

We often only read in textbooks about the stereotypical versions of sexual interests, which presumably separate men and women: that men just want more and more sex with more and more partners (scoring?), that they often have no feelings (for example, tenderness) in the matter, and that they alone are free to pursue and enjoy sex without guilt.[10] On the other side we're told that women suffer the guilt of indiscretions, that they must set the limits against men's advances and deny their own pleasure whether that be autoerotic or interpersonal.

My opinion is that these views should be taken as first approximations at best, and that the real inquiry lies in discovering the many exceptions and actual negotiations to these assumed prescriptions and proscriptions. For example, most of the men I knew in my teens and early adulthood had deep and genuine, even tender, feelings regarding premarital sex and petting, even if not fully expressed or articulated. Men also suffer from guilt, and women do initiate.[11]

From the paradigm (point of view) of men as ever-ready, callous pursuers, it is easy (necessary?) to gloss over or ignore entirely how men actually cope in real life. Certain questions cannot be asked. For example, do men have extended periods of low libido in their lives from time to time? Is there a male menopause? We don't know much about these significant topics.

Rubin[12] has raised the question of sex and personal freedom. In effect she asserts that premodern societies, with fortified households and patri-lineal kinship systems, treat women (and children) as property, especially in the practice of the exchange of wives (exogamous marriages that tend to tie one community together with another), and demand heterosexuality of them. Such practices seem inhumane by today's standards since women have no say in the matter and, by marriage, they may be shipped off to an alien terrain (the husband's community). I'm inclined to agree with her, though I also see that men pay a price in these societies, too, by virtue of military defense for example. That's the nature of these societies. It is not clear that, *at the time* (when one is living *inside* such societies), there is a strong emancipation philosophy, articulated by either women or men for changing the society. Life is geared more toward survival. This is not to say that social change does not occur. It does, but often nonconsciously and from external sources as well as from planned, internal sources.

Also, almost totally neglected in our society is a conversation concerning sexuality and spirituality.[13] In part this topic is blocked out because of our concern with right and wrong (morality) and with technique (notice the many sex manuals and articles in magazines). Several possibilities regarding sex and spirituality can be mentioned. 1) In Tantric Yoga and elsewhere, we have the view that, with proper focus, we can sense something of the transcendental or ecstatic through the rising of sexual energy. Total mobilization of the body, mind, and spirit occurs in a synergy in sharp contrast to the everyday realms of the mundane. These are like "peak experiences." 2) In an insightful way, we can see, through our connection with another's sexuality, the animating persona, which deeply sustains each of us as a human being and gives distinction to our individuality. This can constitute a profound appreciation of another. 3) In the case of sexual addiction, our malady can be seen as pointing to our spiritual poverty. In this way, the addiction is a gift for it draws attention to the "hole" in our being, which can be seen as yearning for the "food" that truly satisfies: our respect for ourselves and our higher power. (More on that later, in Chapters 8 and 9.)

We began this chapter with reference to men's sexual neediness. The question of whether this craving qualifies as an addiction is problematical.[14] Though it seems to be widespread, it is either ignored or taken to be just one of those men's things. In my opinion it deserves compassionate attention and open discussion/research.

Today, much of the attention to male sexuality has been compressed into the negative. In her presidential addresses to the Society for the Scientific Study of Sexuality, Pepper Schwartz asserted recently that male sexuality has been "demonized."[15] However, a feminist rejoinder to my reference to men's sexual craving in this chapter might contend that it is a false, irrelevant, or insignificant issue. For example, even though men in the show-girl club tend to see the performers as being in charge—even powerful—some women, as third parties, might see this situation as scary: an uncovered woman is an unprotected woman, vulnerable and apt to be aggressed against. What is salient to them (many feminists) is the violence of men's sexuality, perpetrated on women against their will. Even the words "male pursuer" may conjure up images to be feared. Men's sexuality is feared, and, in some cases, rightly so. Men must be punished for their sexual crimes and violations. A new subculture for men and between men and women must be created. Men, working "from the heart" with other men (especially older, caring mentors) in men's groups, such as I shall discuss in Chapter 9, can be part of this process.

In Chapter 8, I outline some archtypes. Since they are suggested for use by men, let us apply some here in an illustrative manner to male sexuality. 1) Are men interested in having sex represent or communicate, not just the deep love for their partners, but a "kingly" love that goes out to others around them (in "the kingdom"), inspired by the honor they show each other? 2) Are men willing at times to draw the boundaries of the warrior: for example, No, I'll not accept the sexual invitation of a married woman even though I am attracted to her. 3) Are men willing to bring some of the powers of the magician to bear in sex such that they can hear their partners powerfully and offer understanding. 4) Are men interested in the playfulness of the clown (sex doesn't have to be so serious) and the spontaneity and the endearing self-expression of the wildman.

One of the most interesting views of male/female antipathy, and even violence, is presented by Camille Paglia.[16] Basically, her view is that women are always more powerful than men because they have the secret of life as mistresses of birth. In her libertarian, life-as-guts, pure animal appetite, and gross unpleasantries view, she avers that men's physical attacks on women are their only weapon against a being far more powerful than they.[17] They come out of this wounded desperation and helplessness. In this basic asymmetry of nature (women as the more powerful), men are easily frustrated by their neediness of women's attention, which binds them to women, and their opposite rage for autonomy. She also pushes his buttons of his dependency on her. While not condoning violence, there is, nevertheless, little "inquiry into the sticky complexities of sexual attraction and conflict that implicate *both* partners in any long-running private drama," involving abused and battered women, according to Paglia.[18] He is addicted to her attention and consolation, and she to his apology when she refuses to fight back.

At the same time Paglia commiserates with women against the "facism of nature," which sentences women to procreation or menstruation. She permits women their rebellion with acts such as sodomy and abortion. Abortion *is* killing, (we need to say so), but that's the way life is at times, it's not always tidy and nice, says Paglia. If men don't like women's cock-teasing, that's tough. And if women find themselves in degrading situations at the hands of men, they themselves should take action to reclaim their own dignity, hopefully without special governmental help such as in cases of sexual harassment.

I cannot fully agree. Paglia seems to think that the man/woman war is inevitable. She may not have seen evidence of good men's work. I may be too far out in what I am about to say, but what I see as a possibility among fierce and tender men is that, in initiation, we can create a "male womb" among men into which men can be reconceived and out of which we rebirth them in a profound social, psychological, and spiritual sense. In this, men are brought back up to a par with women (given Paglia's view of women's superiority as the mistresses of birth), and, at the same time, women are honored for their sacrifices of childbearing. I cannot say exactly how this rebirthing of men occurs—just as I cannot fully understand the mystery of the first birth out of women—but I have seen it and experienced it. More will be said in Chapters 8 and 9.

NOTES AND REFERENCES

1. See Randall Collins and Scott Coltrane, *Sociology of Marriage and the Family* (Chicago: Nelson-Hall, 1991), 120–153.

2. Alfred C. Kinsey, Wardell B. Pomeroy, and Clyde E. Martin, *Sexual Behavior in the Human Male* (Philadelphia: Saunders, 1948). Also, *Sexual Behavior in the Human Female*, same authors and publisher, 1953.

3. William Masters and Virginia Johnson, *Human Sexual Inadequacy* (Boston: Little, Brown, 1970).

4. Warren Farrell, *Why Men Are the Way They Are* (New York: McGraw-Hill, 1986), 132–133.

5. See Alice H. Eagly, Antonio J. Mladinic, and Stacy Otto, "Are Women Evaluated More Favorably than Men?" *Psychology of Women Quarterly* 15 (June, 1991), 203–216.

6. Admittedly, the exotic dancer is a blend of both bad and good.

7. I do not wish to overstate a bad/good dichotomy between excitement and passion. If I were to select a color to represent excitement it would be red, for it seems to vibrate with life (even distorted life), and the blood that sustains it. Fear, which one might color black, often accompanies excitement. Both excitement and fear have some potentially redeeming value. Excitement may be transformed into true desire (or passion), as in the desire to seek God or to bring our lives into a more empowered state. Fear,

on the other hand, may sometimes tell us what to stay away from for our own good.

8. John Lee, *At My Father's Wedding* (New York: Bantam, 1991).

9. There is also some research that indicates that men fall in love earlier than women, and that their survival when a romantic relationship breaks up is more problematical. See Sharon S. Brehm, *Intimate Relationships* (New York: Random House, 1985), 102.

10. One of the most glaring examples of this, again, comes from Clyde W. Franklin II. From his article, "The Male Sex Drive," it is not clear whether he is describing how men are *supposed* to act sexually or how they *do* in fact act, but a quote is in order: "In general, men's preoccupation with their penis and (quick) sexual climax and men's compartmentalization of sex preclude their having a specifically chosen sexual relationship that is characterized by deep involvement (with a woman)." He also suggests that men can't be dominant, a very deep need of the "male sex role," according to Franklin, if they get involved with their partners. (This article is published in Laurel Richardson and Verta Taylor, eds., *Feminist Frontiers II* [New York: Random House, 1986], 274–278.) It, the article, is said to be reprinted from Clyde W. Franklin, *The Changing Definition of Masculinity* (New York: Plenum Press, 1984), but, when I compared the article with its cited original source, I found many changes and omissions. The piece has been subsequently dropped in Richardson and Taylor's new *Feminist Frontiers III* (New York: McGraw-Hill, Inc., 1993). Again, I would supplement Franklin's approach (the "control" that the male sex role/s have over men) with a communicative approach, simply, to the effect of: Are the partners willing to communicate to each other what, in the sexual encounter, each likes?

11. See Clinton J. Jesser, "Male Responses to Direct Verbal Sexual Initiatives of Females," *The Journal of Sex Research* 14 (May, 1978), 118–128.

12. Gayle Rubin, "The Traffic in Women: Notes on the Political Economy of Sex," in Rayna Reiter, ed., *Toward an Anthropology of Women* (New York: Monthly Review Press, 1975), 157–210.

13. For example, Masters, Johnson, and Kolodny's new book makes no mention of this topic despite claiming (on the dust jacket) to be "comprehensive." See William H. Masters, Virginia E. Johnson, and Robert C. Kolodny, *Heterosexuality* (New York: HarperCollins, 1994).

14. See Master and Johnson, 224–227.

15. "The Politics of Desire," *Playboy* 53 (June, 1994), 53. By "demonized," she meant that it is stereotypically seen as dangerous and destructive.

16. *Vamps and Tramps* (New York: Vintage Books, 1994).

17. Paglia, 43.

18. Paglia, 43 (italics hers).

Chapter 6

Fatherhood

Fatherhood is a topic critically important to men. An historical coverage is beyond the scope of this chapter.[1] Fatherhood in our society, especially in popular conversation seems to be bifurcated: there are *good* fathers—those who go to work, take care of and recreate with their children, and do housework—and *bad* fathers—those who are selfish, leave their children, booze too much, inflict violence on others, or who fail at or eschew jobs. Fatherhood, in the United States, is a quite common experience: about 85 percent of adult men eventually marry, and about 85 percent of these eventually have children.[2] A sizeable percentage of men are also involved in procreation out-of-wedlock, and most of these cannot be tied to these births as fathers. Yet, among both husbands and wives, fewer are seeing the role of parenthood positively (rewarding, pleasant or easy?) while most still believe it to be "very important."[3]

The exigencies of fatherhood change with the times and are deeply affected by social class factors as well. Fatherhood must also be understood with reference to motherhood, and to the changing cultures of children in mass society as well. Motherhood enjoyed a rosy revival after World War II, when men returned from military service, and moms were encouraged to take up fulltime (professional) homemaking in the emerging suburban family.[4] But, many women, especially in the middle class, found that life-style unfulfilling. Many, out of choice or necessity, began to enter (re-enter) the paid labor force. Yet, the maternal mystique—the idea that the mother-infant bond is crucial to healthy infant development, or that mothers, not fathers, are uniquely suited to raising children—took firm hold in the American consciousness.[5] Some other developments in American society affecting the opportunities, variations, and character of fathering should be mentioned. First, there are the factors associated with the shrinking family unit itself. Birth rates, except for the 1950s, have been coming down, due, in part, to increases in urbanization, job expansion, contraception, and delayed age of marriage. The family became a smaller, more nucleated, mobile unit. This means men will be fathers to fewer children. At the same time, the desired relationship between spouses moved toward the "companionate" type, meaning toward partners being more equalitarian.[6] It also means that, without ready help from extended kin or neighbors, the one spouse must be ready to fill in for the other when necessary. Additionally, in spite of the fact that goods once produced largely in the household, such as food and clothing, can now be purchased, and labor-saving devices and low-maintenance houses are available, the modern family seems to be as busy a place as ever—even harried in the pressure on time. And, housework tended to come out with a very low rating in the score-keeping of the feminism of the sixties through nineties.[7]

Two other factors must be mentioned as background here: work (jobs) and divorce. Until recently, most fathers expected to be the primary breadwinner in their families, and, for most of those men, the amount of time available to spend with children was loosely, inversely related to the amount of time they spent on the job and traveling to and from the job. Generally, this still gave them access to children, for marriage and parenthood were well connected. Rising divorce rates have changed all that. At the same time that more fathers are getting involved with their children in their households (especially those putting in less time on jobs), the number of father-absent living units with little children in them is growing, mostly because of divorce and the assignment of custody to the mother in nine out of ten cases.[8]

A number of new and significant research studies have emerged in the last few years. Two in particular are noteworthy here. The first is an interesting study by Kathleen Gerson, which consisted of interviews with a non-statistically representative sample of 138 men from the New York metropolitan area. Some of the men chosen at random for the study were taken from an alumni list of a private university, and some (more working class), from a list of workers maintained by a labor council. Their average age was thirty-six, and sixty percent were married, 11 percent divorced or widowed, and 29 percent had never married. Almost one-half of those who were married had wives who were employed full time, and 53 percent had at least one child.[9]

Gerson's analysis centers on the ways men turn to or find themselves in breadwinning (being the sole or primary financial support for the family), autonomy (did not become a parent or had become estranged from one's children), or involved fatherhood (child care-taking as well as economic support). Roughly, she found about one-third of the men in each of the three categories, but it was the dynamics of how men came into these categories that enlivens this study. Some men turned, reluctantly, toward breadwinning because they found unexpected job stability/opportunity, unexpected marital commitment after the marriage began, unexpected parenthood, or they developed a commitment before marriage began to a woman who preferred to be a domestic partner.[10] Other breadwinners began their adult lives already in that orientation and remained there at the time of the study.

Major factors that played into men turning from breadwinner toward autonomy were also interesting: some were frustrated with work (for example, the regimentation work routines imposed on the rest of their life, the unwelcomed supervision they received at work, or the competition on the job). Some of these men actively avoided marriage or were unable to attract a desirable mate; others experienced traumatic or disillusioning events, which propelled them out of relationships, and, corollary, away from a commitment to support a woman; some now autonomous fathers blamed unfair judges, a biased court system, and angry wives for their postdivorce plight, and they, consequently, lost interest in supporting[11]; some became autonomous due to childlessness, while others took this route because of the perceived excessive demands of children.

Finally, there are the men who were both economic supporters and involved fathers. Several factors played into the determination of this position according to Gerson. Some voluntarily switched to less demanding jobs even at lower pay; others found themselves blocked to upward job mobility.[12] Most of these men were married to women who had or were embarking on promising careers. In a few cases these involved fathers' contribution to childcare/housework exceeded those of their wives, but in most cases the working wives' contributions still exceeded those of the involved fathers.

Involved fathers attempted to limit or manage the demands of parenthood by keeping the family small or using paid or unpaid help when possible.[13] Those involved fathers who resisted full equality—Gerson calls them "mother's helpers"—often avoided some dirty work (for example, getting up at night for the child) or taking over-all direction for the child. Nonetheless, most of these men, says Gerson, made tough decisions in laying claim to parental involvement (some 30 percent of the breadwinners who had flexible time to do more parenting did not[14]) and a full 74 percent reported parental involvement as "fulfilling," a much higher percentage than for the men in the other two categories.[15] Unfortunately, when a few fathers moved toward support/involvement, their wives divorced them. Interestingly, these men tended to have better postdivorce relations with their children, in part, due to her (mothers') career aspirations or desire for freedom.[16]

Another study, this one by Snarey, takes us into the enriching interpersonal realm of fathers and their children, into that which Erik Erikson called "generativity."[17] This study has the virtue of longitudinality, a follow through of the same men over a forty-year time period. It scrutinizes these men's "caring activities which create or contribute to the life of the next generation."[18] It sees how healthy men *want* to give to their children and, at the same time, how they (the men) receive satisfaction in return. The study makes some much needed distinctions into the many *types* of generative-help men can give to children at various stages in the child's life, but suffers from a lack of coverage of the resources—time, money, job, expertise—men need to possess in order to generate.

EVALUATION

More studies could be reviewed, but we have the basis for some evaluation in reference to some salient men's issues.

Some feminist rhetoric of the past has tended to see some men's/women's issues as a zero-sum game. That is, the idea that the more one side won, the more the other lost. Therefore, it was hard to discuss men's rights (since men were already assumed to possess the advantage in privileges) without implying a subtraction in women's rights. In this regard Gerson's report is interesting. In the introduction she states: "There are inherent perils in any analysis of men. Since they are members of an advantaged group that still enjoys disproportionate power and privilege, it is necessary (if difficult) to strike a balance between sympathetic understanding of the problems men face and appropriate awareness of their uses and misuses of power . . . (as feminists) . . . We cannot completely set aside our personal experiences . . . "[19] Yet, Gerson goes on to defend men's veracity (on a par with women's), to explore how men's lives are shaped and to "search for signs of positive change as well as signs that change is limited or harmful."[20] Not bad! She is in good company here, in my opinion, in both the value and the necessity of having men speak for themselves.[21]

There is still something more important in her book, regarding the contentious question of the overload of wives' labor compared to husbands': " . . . And when the time spent performing paid work, housework, and child care is added together, men work an average of eighty-eight fewer hours a year than do women."[22] This is, to me, astounding. Assuming her figures are accurate, are we really doing battle between the sexes over what computes down to less than two hours per week more labor for women?

Finally, one more issue noted by Gerson: "Numerous studies have noted that when divorced fathers are estranged from their children or from decisions about their children's lives, they are likely to withhold or withdraw economic support as well. By allowing and encouraging fathers' participation, we increase the chances that children will also receive economic support."[23] Well said. The number of deadbeat fathers might be smaller than public (political) attention indicates.

It is quite clear that if given the time, the opportunity, and the encouragement, men can nurture and take care of children effectively, even to reconcile the pressure to be both the disciplinarian and the friend to the children. They must also have good information about child-rearing. In this regard Griswold, who presents a history of fatherhood in America, discusses, among other developments, the rise of the "therapeutic culture" of child-rearing. This included the deluge of advice from doctors, psychologists, and educators, starting about fifty years ago in our society, to parents regarding the intricacies of raising (and controlling) kids in these confusing times. This development has become big business; but, says Griswold, "The critical point for our purpose is that this culture was not built by experts alone but by *mothers* and experts together."[24] Fathers were left out. Of course, there is no point in ascribing simply monetary motives to the experts or pernicious motives to the mothers. Child-rearing *is* difficult and, oftentimes, bewildering. Help is needed. But we must seek to include men. Indeed, what I hear from the fathers, in the many men's groups I have been in, is their deep concern to do the best for their children. I also see that when men are acknowledged for what they *do right* as a father (even if it is only a little), they are often refreshed and empowered.

New family-support policies (flex-time, paternity leaves, or more accessible/affordable daycare for children) will be needed. Fathers' rights groups will also persist in their efforts for divorced men to have custody consideration, shared parenting, access (to children) enforcement, and fair child-support laws. Welfare policies may also need to be scrutinized for poor or disabled men with dependent children. Good fathers are needed—especially by sons.[25]

In conclusion, I would like to return to the concerns of Osherson in Chapter 4, especially to the issue of fathers and failure. Much of the research centers on fathers who have *difficulties*—what about those who have deep wounds, and the cycle of woundedness has been going on many generations in the kinship line. One of the most sobering studies I have ever encountered has been written recently by Lansky.[26] Though it is written from a non-sociological point of view (we don't learn much about the men's demographic backgrounds, for example) and in a language of psychiatry that is technically opaque to ordinary readers, it contains some very blunt admissions:

Years of clinical experience with a wide range of psychiatrically impaired fathers have convinced me that these men will talk about almost anything rather than admit these failures at fathering. They complain of 'voices' of suicidality. They admit to substance abuse, domestic violence, even homicide. They acknowledge failures on jobs, in marriages, and in relation to their families of origin. But they will do almost anything rather than face their failures as fathers . . . When circumstances or family members confront the father with his failure and the consequences of that failure . . . the usual result is a state of shameful futility that is like no other anguish imaginable. That anguish is often unbearable to witness even by seasoned professionals . . . [27]

If men's groups do nothing else, they might be worthwhile as a place where men can "hear" that shame, and support its healing. For us men who are less psychiatrically impaired than those dealt with by Lansky, and there are millions, if we have a safe place in which to acknowledge our faults, and the courage to make amends where possible, we shall have laid some new track for generations to come. Fierce and Tender are our names.

NOTES AND REFERENCES

1. See Robert L. Griswold, *Fatherhood in America: A History* (New York: Basic Books, 1993).

2. See John Snarey, *How Fathers Care for the Next Generation* (Cambridge, Mass.: Harvard University, 1993), 32. I have revised his citation downward by 5 percent.

3. Griswold, 229.

4. See Betty Friedan, *The Feminine Mystique* (New York: W. W. Norton and Company, Inc., 1963).

5. See Richard A. Warshak, *The Custody Revolution* (New York: Poseidon Press, 1992), part 1.

6. See, for example, Marcia Lasswell and Thomas Lasswell, *Marriage and the Family* (Belmont, Calif.: Wadsworth, 1991), 218–225.

7. See Alice Abel Kemp, *Women's Work: Degraded and Devalued* (Englewood Cliffs, N.J.: Prentice-Hall, 1994), especially Chapter 8.

8. See Mary Ann Schwartz and Barbara Marliene Scott, *Marriages and Families* (Englewood Cliffs, N.J.: Prentice-Hall, 1994), 369.

9. Kathleen Gerson, *No Man's Land: Men's Changing Commitments to Family and Work* (New York: Basic Books, 1993), 10–11.

10. Gerson, 77–104.

11. Gerson, 110–138.

12. Gerson, 143–150.

13. Gerson, 219–226.

14. Gerson, 235.

15. Gerson, 324.

16. Gerson, 170–171.

17. Snarey, 18, 19.

18. Snarey, 14.

19. Gerson, 12.

20. Gerson, 12.

21. Judith A. Seltzer and Yvonne Brandreth make a similar point in "What Fathers Say About Involvement with Children After Separation," *Journal of Family Issues* 15 (March, 1994), 59.

22. Gerson, 5, 6.

23. Gerson, 315.

24. Griswold, 126, emphasis mine.

25. Griswold, 234–236. Recently, I noticed and joined the National Fatherhood Initiative, which is new, and which has an illustrious list of names on its advisory board. Among its goals: to make responsible fatherhood a national priority. Among its statistics is this one: Tonight, almost 40 percent of America's children will go to sleep in the house where their biological father does not live.

26. Melvin R. Lansky, *Fathers Who Fail: Shame and Psychopathology in the Family System* (Hillsdale, N.J.: The Analytic Press, 1992).

27. Lansky, 8. Also see Roy U. Schenk and John Everingham, eds., *Men Healing Shame* (New York: Springer Publishing Company, 1995).

Chapter 7

Men and Work

Up to this point we've not said much about work in this book. Now is a good time since financial success for a man has been stressed, and work is usually a prerequisite to that. Most Americans are not independently wealthy. They must work to make a livelihood, and, increasingly over the last one hundred years, as the number of self-owned farms and businesses has declined, they work for large employers away from their homes. Roughly 65 percent of women and 85 percent of men ages eighteen to forty-nine are employed in this way.[1]

Work has many faces,[2] there is a great variety of jobs and professions in modern society. We do, however, find a paradox regarding employment: on the one hand, Americans say it is good to work and, consequently, many say they would still work even if they won the lottery; on the other hand, many say they would change jobs if they could—that their work is not satisfying to them.

People work for several major reasons: 1) for survival, 2) for autonomy (for example, to have money so one can do more as one pleases), 3) for self-validation (I'm a competent person because I do this kind of work), and 4) for maintaining one's connection to life—to stay in the mainstream.

Most men believe they have little or no option regarding work— they must do so. Most adult men are married and, therefore, have others who depend on them for support to some degree. Most states, until recently, had asymmetrical support laws, which said in effect that it was the duty of the *husband* to support the wife (within his means) irrespective of her separate means. Wives had no such obligation under law. Of course most of the rationale for such laws was the idea that wives became mothers, and children needed caretakers; these were preferably the children's mothers. So it was thought best that women should have a prior claim to men's support although, admittedly, such claims are not easy to enforce.

Many middle-class men have good jobs; that is, they pay reasonably well, there is some stability or security (although jobs increasingly disappear at this level, too, lately), the setting of the work is relatively free from hazards, and these men enjoy some creativity and autonomy in their jobs—though many say they are not making the difference for society they'd like.

Their jobs have generally well reflected their status for themselves and their families to the community. And, still, many feel they *should* be doing better—should be *more* successful. Farrell contends that now with more women working and earning more money, there is even more pressure on men since many women feel they must marry *up* (from their own level), which eliminates more men as potential partners.[3]

What I have noticed about the lives of many middle-class married men is that they were stressed by the squeeze for time to do all that was needed, especially if young children were in the family, assistance from relatives was lacking, and both spouses were employed. Many of these men (and, increasingly today, many women as well) have "greedy" jobs—they require a lot of time, preparation, and commitment.[4] There may be insecurity as well, not knowing if one is doing well enough. Men who have remarried after a divorce may have obligations to the previous family members. A full life is very hard to manage: planning time together for the spouses themselves, meeting the needs of children, and the call of organizations (such as church or service groups). Finding any time to spend with other men in a support group such as I will describe later (in Chapter 9) is a great challenge.

For many working-class men, though, the story is quite different. They go directly from high school into the manual labor force and, soon after, get married and start a family.[5] Mortgages and other long-term obligations arise. Job stability is often in doubt; layoffs are always feared. Lack of education often stands in the way of promotion. These men's job activity tends to be closely supervised by the boss, and serious hazards to health may be present in the form of injury or noxious elements in the line of production. The intersections of love, home, and work seem to be constantly strained. (To my knowledge, in the mass media, only country western music or the blues allow the expression of this strain in a realistic way: I came home and my wife and kids were gone; She said I didn't understand her; I'm out of work and I'm on the road again; I'm really hurtin' tonight and I've got only a bottle of whiskey to get me through 'til the mornin'.)[6]

It is common to misunderstand the world of work and the economic behavior of men, especially of those men in the near-poor ranks. As children, growing up in struggling families with low economic means, we learn that decisions are serious—that if we make the wrong one it could cost us dearly and there'd be blame and punishment to deal with. I remember that pressure in my family of orientation. Later, in early adulthood, I tended to perpetuate the pattern. I thought I had to control economic resources closely—by myself. I even questioned (doubted) my decisions, which turned out later to be very good ones. The point to be understood is that when people are poor there is very little margin for error; backup cushions are lacking such as we find for higher middle-class families and above.[7] For this reason, decisions are riskier among poorer people and even guarding/controlling behavior that looks irrational from an upper middle-class vantage—like hanging on to a dead-end job—is normal. Such behavior may even continue once a more comfortable station in life is attained.

The importance of work to a man's life should not be underestimated. Sometimes, it may, indeed, be a diversion from what is going on inside of him (for example, grief) that he needs to confront, and sometimes work is something we need in order to maintain our sense of worth and value. In "olden times," some men's work also gave them their mission in the sense that they could see their work contributing to the well-being of the community, and it might have been so acknowledged by others as well. For many men that sense of leadership for the collective good in one's work is missing today.

Sometimes major dislocations occur to a society or a community. This was the case for the many men and women I lived among on the Pine Ridge Indian Reservation. One hundred and eighty years ago, they were still a proud and relatively self-sufficient people. To be sure, from our perspective today, hardships and deprivations existed then— theirs wasn't an idyllic life. But today the devastation on the reservation is clear. Especially the men are missing. *Where are they?* I asked. The answer came in bits and pieces: some had migrated, often temporarily, to cities in search of jobs outside of the reservation; some were in prison or on the lam; some died early from disease, accidents, violence (including suicide), and war. Unemployment on the reservation was at least 80 percent; and among those men that remained, alcoholism rates were high.

To be sure, many women's lives were seriously troubled too, but there were more of them around, and many of them were doing a valiant job with the home and survival. What disturbed me was the total picture of oppression, neglect, and dejection, but in particular the failure of officials to ask, What about the men? What can be done? Many seemed to think the men were just lost. When the men sometimes acted macho, there was little interest in the possibility of asking, Could this be an expression of their lack of generativity? In this case, their inability to receive dignity in roles played for the good of the community?[8]

Today we may be entering another major—this time, worldwide dislocation; the job signs look frightening to many people, even the middle class. Unemployment has been inching up in many of the previously prosperous countries of Europe—10 percent to 20 percent is now tolerated. Economists talk about the dual-labor force, consisting of core jobs in big (relatively noncompetitive) industries, which pay fairly well and seem to entail some security, and peripheral jobs which are low wage and more subject to layoffs as markets shrink or change even temporarily. What I am saying is that more of us may be moving to the periphery category, in which case, it is hoped, a cross-national dialogue may take place around the question, How do people get the resources they need to maintain a livelihood, especially when unemployed? and How do men exercise their desire to lead for the good of the community? This should be treated as a structural problem of modern societies.

According to our Protestant work ethic, each of us alone is responsible before God for our successes *and* failures. All of us are exhorted to work diligently in honest labor. Both middle-class and working-class (and poor) men tend to lack the support groups in which they can talk openly about major events in their lives: paychecks and promotions; risky economic decisions; the fear or impact of infidelity or unemployment; the birth of children; the juggling of schedules and the training for fatherhood; the problems with co-workers or relatives; the children leaving home; the search for meaning in life; and the ravages of illness and ageing. As I shall suggest in Chapters 8 and 9 of this book, there is some real hope for change.

As in all societies, the nature of work has a history, and it is located in the larger setting of social, economic, and political arrangements. Something called "modernity" arose in the West sometime from the thirteenth to the eighteenth centuries. A number of factors were involved: 1) commercial and industrial development—together, with emphasis on capitalism, where private property and individual gain stood as hallmarks—were institutionalized; 2) the securement of peace for market activity within an expanding region by larger, more powerful governments occurred; and 3) the establishment of a scientific point of view with its emphasis on individualism and doubt (let me see for myself), reason, and efficiency began to prevail in all our affairs.[9] The old (solid), moral order became relativistic, and thousands of different voices emerged to be heard from the pluralistic subcultures of diverse peoples and philosophies brought together within this new and ambient community. In people's quest for identity in mass society, these separate ethnic and religious boundaries can also become strongly solidified, and intense antagonisms between them may then be the result.

There are tradeoffs. Many people enjoy the ambience—the old, moral folk-society could be harsh on deviants or nonconformists.

Many like the economy—capitalism, guided by science, tends to be productive, and a higher standard of living together with longevity is possible for more people on a mass scale. But, modern capitalists also tend to become unbalanced as they become larger and loose their visions of *general* social welfare and for the quality of the environment. And, philosophically, by the swords of reason and criticism, we've cracked our "cosmic egg,"[10] the integrated, authoritative, and mystical view of the world we had in olden times. We now have nothing bigger than our little, episodic lives to hatch into or out of. We have our *individual* rights, our *personal* feelings, our suspicions, and things to buy (if we can afford them). And, it is hoped, we're employed or have the means to survive. Is that enough?

In closing this part of this book, and before opening the topics in Chapters 8 and 9, we might make brief reference to the notion of transformation since it is involved, though often unintentionally, in our journey; it is slippery when we try to define it. Transformation is a process generated when quantitative changes produce qualitatively new outcomes. It is something new coming out of the old that is usually not fully anticipated. Karl Marx modeled transformation in stages: thesis (the initial condition or state), antithesis (the forces of change to or in the state), and synthesis (the new state or condition).[11] In human development, transformation often refers to a radical shift in a person's life, which is not fully explicable by the change in his/her outer circumstances. What we would like to do in men's work is produce transformation *intentionally* and for positive ends.

Initiation, as I am conceiving of it, may be viewed as a conscious transformative process. In order to see some of its distinct elements, I would like to contrast initiation with a process called brainwashing.[12] Brainwashing is a term that became popular after it was discovered that U.S. soldiers, returning from North Korean prison camps in the 1950s, seemingly had undergone a radical alteration in personality and view of the world. Quantitative change seemed to add up to a qualitatively radical outcome. As researchers have examined this process in retrospect, we see some of the secrets that promote these dramatic cases of brainwashing: 1) the subject (prisoner) is isolated in a camp cut off from outside influences and contacts; 2) he is stripped of amenities and becomes totally dependent on his fellow prisoners, especially on those who are making progress in the retraining program, and on the superiors who run the camp; 3) his previous identity (who he was, what he stood for) is denigrated—hazing occurs, and humiliation is the result; 4) he is "told," by instructions, by stories, and by example, what is expected of him as a subject in terms of new values and goals and he is punished for his nonconformity; 5) he is gradually required to expend energy or endure some hardship for the good of the group (for example, clean rest rooms, wash clothes); 6) public confessions before the group are required in which the subject admits his previous faulty deeds and ways of thinking and indicates how he is now changing and correcting these; and 7) later, at appropriate times in his rehabilitation, ceremonies of recognition are held in his honor as a visible means of marking his progress or arrival to his new status as an insider.

When my students in introductory sociology hear of this process, they usually recoil in horror—morally it is offensive. I agree. Then I ask them to see whether elements of brainwashing may not be present in (familiar) situations—family, sorority/fraternity inductions, new recruits to seminaries and the military for example—albeit in a milder, more voluntaristic manner. They usually can see that, and they are usually surprised to find it.

Initiation is crucial to a man's life in my opinion. It may happen unintentionally or intentionally. It may occur dramatically in a time-place situation or more gradually over a series of events over the years. I see that some elements of brainwashing are present in initiation especially in the intentional case—some isolation of the initiate may occur, hardships are endured, stories in which exemplary models to be emulated are told, speaking of wounds is shared in front of the group, and a point occurs, usually with a ceremony, which marks a transition to a new status and identity.

But there are some very important differences: 1) usually the initiate calls *himself* forth into the process very voluntarily—he offers himself, empty or naked, in the face of the unknown into which he will venture, 2) leaders are not superiors, but mentors who have come through the process themselves, and 3) mentors are less interested in obedience to a party line than to the welfare of the boy's soul—that is, they solemnly bless the boy on his journey, and (in the words of Michael Meade), will see to it that the heat of initiation is neither too hot or too cold.

So while the boy is held in this container of love and challenge by his elders, and at certain points, may join his peers in activities designed to instill trust, he is essentially on his own to find his inner, fierce and tender energies, his higher power and mission. Paradoxically, it is the wounds, past and present, which are the basis of the initiatory process, and, if properly handled, allow a boy (man) to reclaim his life and press it into service for the good of the community. A type of rebirth occurs and involves what a man does with and learns from his losses, as well as what he gains from myth and other men regarding who he is, and how he can make and take a stand. To this adventure we now turn; onto this court we now step.

EVALUATION

It is not my intention to belittle the lives of the many women who work both inside the home and outside, by option and necessity. Nor is it my intention to slight the many women who seek work or higher paying, more prestigious jobs and encounter barriers not applied to men. The 1964 Civil Rights Act began addressing some of these problems and more needs to be done. Sexual harassment on the job needs also to be continually addressed.[13]

Instead, I would emphasize some salient concerns of men: employment and unemployment, hazards (for example, toxins or accidents) and debasement in many jobs, pressures for more success, and difficulties in negotiating home/work demands for those with children (which still receives little attention in the marriage/family textbooks). What is of special concern is the sense of burden many men feel as the one who has no option not to work, as the one who can make no financial mistakes. Lillian Rubin writes poignantly of this experience when she and her husband seriously switched roles.[14]

Also, as work became rationalized in the modern world, productivity took on the characteristics of calculated efficiency and controlled repetition. Men felt most of the brunt of this. It is debilitating to the human spirit. To the degree that men must give themselves to their work, they must ignore their feelings and desires. The economic machine simply grinds them down, even in enlightened workplaces. A community into which a man's efforts contribute, and where they can be acknowledged, is also importantly missing in today's world.

Men in men's groups can partially compensate for this as they take on missions or as they find (or are coached by other men into finding) ways to redesign their work so as to make a difference for themselves and others. For example, a number of years ago I was feeling the deadening routinization of my university teaching in spite of the fact that, fortunately, I hold a rather creative job. With coaching from others, I was able to redesign how I taught, but I also changed my teaching so as to involve students more, even to the point where they could define some projects for themselves, use the concepts and theories of the course to carry those out or evaluate them, and receive part of their final grade on that process. (See Chapter 9.) I realize that men (and women) in other occupations may be more restricted in the changes they can produce.

For the last four years, I have been attending open AA meetings. It is here that I was reminded of the central life obligation work is among the men who spoke. Many of them also shared that being denied a job after applying for one can be a very devastating experience. Several men observed that without the support of other men in the program, after such repeated rejections, they might well have given up and returned to drinking. But these are recovering alcoholics we might note. I wonder how much different job rejections are for other men as well?

NOTES AND REFERENCES

1. See Jean Stockard and Miriam M. Johnson, *Sex and Gender in Society* (Englewood Cliffs, N.J.: Prentice-Hall, 1992), 27–34.

2. See Studs Terkel, *Working* (New York: Avon Books, 1972).

3. Warren Farrell, *Why Men Are the Way They Are* (New York: McGraw-Hill, 1986), 171.

4. Recently, it was reported that Americans are working, on average, 160 hours per year *more* in 1990 than in 1970. This is in sharp contrast to

the dominant conversation of the 1960s, when it was believed that, due to the cybernetic revolution (and computer chip), more leisure was going to be available to all.

5. See Lillian Breslow Rubin, *Worlds of Pain* (New York: Basic Books, 1976), Chapter 5.

6. An interesting article appears in *Newsweek* (March 29, 1993), 48–53, entitled, "White Male Paranoia" by David Gates. In this article, Gates asserts the usual fare: white males are confused and threatened because the numbers of minorities in the population are rising, new job-hiring policies are in effect, sexual harassment charges multiply against them, and voices from gays and women speak disparagingly of them. What's particularly interesting about the author's analysis is how he jumps from discussions of beleaguered middle-class and near-poor men, whose incomes dropped 25 percent during the 1980s, to the *collective* characteristics of white men as a whole category (82.5 percent of the Forbes 400 are *white men*, 77 percent of congress) to imply that *all* men are still overprivileged.

Furthermore, there is more than a hint of a long-standing upper middle-class snobbery (from both men and women) toward less-educated men when the author asserts that "White males voted 62 to 37 percent against Clinton . . . partly out of fear that his multicultural ecofeminist storm troopers would take away their guns, steaks, cigarettes, V-8 engines—and jobs." I wonder why we regard the men who pick up our garbage, roof our houses, and drive our taxicabs that way? As an aside, I can say that I was born of very poor parents, and I was thirty-five years old before I learned that there was a financial vehicle known as a family trust fund. Many of my upper middle-class female (and male) friends not only knew of them, but went to elite colleges from their proceeds.

Finally, let me say that recently a friend of mine opened an agency for mediation of (largely) divorce and postdivorce (coparenting) issues. To his surprise, hundreds of near-poor men swamped his office with grievances. They felt that "regular" agencies and the courts gave them little protection, justice, or services and, besides, they couldn't afford the fees.

7. See Rubin, Chapter 9.

8. A very similar position is taken by Maxine Baca Zinn, "Chicano Men and Masculinity," *The Journal of Ethnic Studies*, 10 (Summer, 1982), 29–44.

9. See Irving M. Zeitlin, *Ideology and the Development of Sociological Theory* (Englewood Cliffs, N.J.: Prentice-Hall, 1987), 150–161.

10. See Joseph Chilton Pearce, *The Crack in the Cosmic Egg* (New York: The Julian Press, 1988).

11. See Karl Marx, *The Communist Manifesto* (Chicago: Henry Regnery Co., 1954).

12. See Robert Jay Lifton, *Thought Reform and the Psychology of Totalism* (New York: W. W. Norton, 1961).

13. See Barbara F. Reskin and Irene Padioic, *Women and Men at Work* (Thousand Oaks, Calif.: Pine Forge Press, 1994).

14. Lillian B. Rubin, *Intimate Strangers* (New York: Harper and Row, 1983), 22–24.

PART III

Coming Together for Healing and Action

Chapter 8

Finding the Father: Creating a Stand

Robert Bly was, until recently, mainly known for his poetry. He grew up in the north country of Madison, Minnesota, born, as he says it, into a Norwegian, Lutheran family whose father was an alcoholic. His grasp of fairy tales, stories, and myths from around the world, in different cultures and in history from the early civilizations to the present, is rich and wonderful.

Bly came to the attention of many men outside the circles of poetry in 1982 in an interview article titled "What Men Really Want."[1] He has since written other pieces of great interest, especially his *Iron John*.[2] For lack of a better word, we call his teaching "mythopoetic." His ideas or coaching are not easily summarized. Scientists tend to write in carefully defined concepts guided by falsifiable hypotheses rigorously investigated. Not Robert Bly. He reads a poem, tells a story, weeps and dances with men.

At a recent men's gathering, Bly started his presentation with these words: "There's a feeling all over the culture that the mythology we have isn't answering anymore." By this he means that our lives are no longer connected in a satisfying way, that vision and passion are missing. Myths[3] give the water of life to a whole group, yet we're in the desert. More on that later. Here are Bly's guiding ideas as I find them, written in my own words:

1. Within the last three hundred years, the structure of life in the West has changed dramatically. Industrialization and rational/modern developments are the main sources of this axial change.

2. Modernity means a sharp break from the past. Fathers (and many mothers) have left the home to work as cottage industry gave way to the office, business, and factory in a market economy. Most children began to see their fathers for a very short time each day; and child-rearing, except for the upper classes, rested mainly with mothers who did the best they could.

3. Out of secular rationality—the worship of efficiency, high productivity, and the compartmentalization of life—organic groupings of kin, neighborhoods, apprenticeships, began to disappear, and rituals, particularly male-initiation rituals, were abandoned. The enchantment of storytelling by the old men for the young men vanished, too. Our closeness to the earth and its cycles[4] and creatures slipped away. Social stratification intensified, and many men began to see themselves as failures.

4. Official Policy ignored that which we disliked about ourselves: characteristics that in irresponsibility—and as propaganda—got projected onto others (for example, those communists or, now, those damned Japanese). These Bly calls "shadows."

5. As a result of the absence of fathers and the lack of pride and vision in fathers, sons have been unsupported—this is the essential wound in men's lives today.

6. Out of this father absence many difficulties arise, among them the continued rivalry between cross-gender partners (husbands and wives) as though they were siblings, and a loss of the male mode of feeling—men's distrust of their own perceptions and experience, which often get channeled as the young men's suspicion and harsh criticism of the older men. True mentorship is missing.

7. Few men are "twice born" (not Bly's term); that is, few have come through initiation with clear older men in a deliberate and caring ordeal.[5] Young men tend then to fit various undeveloped types, among them: a) the flying men/boys who whistle over the top of the wound, often having grandiose plans, which never get completed; these men don't stay focused; b) the rough men/boys who act with bravado and inflict their wound on others and must get what they want; c) men/boys who show very little feeling at all; d) men/boys who have weak boundaries, who are sensitive, but easily pushed over, easily hurt, too agreeable, snared into helping everyone else out of

their troubles; e) lost men/boys who are passive and who have lit direction on their own; and f) Preening men/boys.

8. The road back for men does not begin with shaming men or recounting their defects, but by entering their sorrow—going *down* into the wound (for which, in this society, there is little support) and finding a garden, a sanctuary where they can be safe and regroup. A man will experience his authentic feminine through his masculine only once there is a pride and identification with the latter.

9. In his journey of recovery, a man may go through certain noticeable stages: a) a break from his mother or other women on whom he had grown dependent, such as for approval, or for whom he needs to do good works or on whom he depends to absorb or explore his feelings; b) the discovery of a male-mother—another man who cares about him; c) an engagement with his own external biological father, saying goodbye to him, and the bringing forth of his own internal father, often in the company of other men.

10. A man may be said to have several levels of cathexes (again, this is not Bly's term): needs, wants, and desires. Twice-born men especially operate a great deal from desires. Desires speak from our deeper calling into life—often remembered from when we were altruistic, unstoppable children. Usually desires cannot be completely fulfilled, but they keep stretching us to what's beyond reasonable. More on this in the next chapter.

11. Since feelings and sensibilities of men may need to be addressed differently than women's, very different stories filled with metaphor and archetypes may speak powerfully to men (see Meade in the references). Archetypes, according to C. G. Jung, are impersonal, innate patterns (images) that prompt our ways of feeling, thinking, and doing. They belong to the collective unconscious of all human beings and those archetypes to which Bly and others (especially Moore and Gillette[6]) have paid particular attention are the king, the clown, the magician, the warrior, the lover, and the wildman.[7]

None of these archetypes should be treated as doctrinal categories. They are flexible and spongy. In discussing them here I am not at all suggesting a return to some (falsely) idealized society of the past. Instead they can be used in different ways by different men (and women) in their lives in today's world. At most we can say something about the general energy to which they point—the possibilities their denotations and connotations open up.

ˡomain, a realm. He brings order. He draws
ates a sense of mission, and gives generously.
are of all in his heart, empowers their creativity, and
with healing compassion and admiration. The distorted
ˌ king uses people for his own power, or he acts helpless when
on is needed. *The clown* is our respite from surplus seriousness.
He's a zany trickster. He honors the king and vice versa. I found that
many men who are very busy in their lives have almost lost touch
entirely with their clown and realize that they have little inclination
to play, be silly, or just dawdle. *The magician* can detach from and
transcend the ordinary. He can make outrageous declarations that
change the nature of our reality: Maybe I'll just turn you into a frog!
The magician offers us clarity, understanding, and reflection since he
can see issues from many different perspectives. Like a prophet of old,
he can stand up and confront the distorted king chiding him for his
errant path. He is also able to handle psychological forces, and, as a
mentor, helps us to tap the inner knowledge that gives us power to do
good for the whole kingdom. We all need the magician; many of us
are in our heads, but locked out of our minds—someone told us long
ago that we are dumb and we unfortunately believed him or her. The
negative magician always makes others wrong, or he has no feeling
whatsoever.

The warrior was already eluded to in earlier chapters. He is no
warrior at all unless he *serves* the (his) king. He defends his boundaries:
You can't talk like that to me anymore; or I won't loan you any more
money. Again, creating healthy boundaries may include *himself*. I
won't talk like that to her anymore. He takes out his sword and says,
That's enough! He puts the doorknob of his door to his life on the
inside of the door. He also makes commitments and takes a stand. The
warrior ventures into where it is dangerous, knowing the difference
between foolish (ego) bravery and the cause of the king. He's safe for
women to be with because he has dared to own his rage, go to the
bottom of it, and transform it into clear anger out of which healthy
boundaries are drawn (see the next chapter). He can take a stand for
his own self-esteem. The warrior also brings forth the strength to finish
a difficult project like writing this book. He has learned a craft for his

own support. The warrior is soft *and* hard, gentle *and* fierce. He'll ask a woman to go with him only when he knows where *he* is going in life. The warrior acts decisively and directly (frontally). He creates life as choices. The warrior can also help a man bring out his witch in order to speak up when others are going along with just being nice, when, in fact, an unpopular wake-up call is needed for all.

The distorted warrior has been well summarized recently by Keen: "The neophyte warrior learns to disdain woman's ways. . . . to deny all that is feminine and soft in himself."[8] Also, "The warrior's body is perpetually uptight and ready to fight."[9] The false warrior has (ego) pride and quarrelsomeness, which are okay if he's going to learn from these. He can see things only as black or white. He puts up walls instead of boundaries. When he's ticked off, neither you nor he know where or how he's going to come down. He is capable of hideous cruelties. He hasn't gone into his sorrow nor faced his shadows.

The *lover* has passion. He can extend his emotion in the area of his efforts and appreciations. He cares about others. He can look into a woman's eyes and see if the window of her heart is open and then honor her. He has vision and sensuality—he can make a commitment *and* feel the pleasure of physical intertwinement. The lover is also a dreamer, but is not snarled into his emotions or immobilized by the objects of his love. The lover humanizes the other archetypes and gives connectivity to life. The distorted lover frets when she doesn't make him happy anymore and then he looks for someone new.

The *wildman* is a wonderful archetype. In the fairy tale, "Iron John," he's found in the dark at the bottom of the pond. He's hairy and untamed. He represents the spontaneity we've lost in life as we've boxed ourselves into being nice guys and as we've accumulated mort-gages. The wildman brings us back to glories and wisdom of nature, to all living things and their cycles, to the wind, the sun, the water, the mountains. He carries a lot of good feminine energy. These archetypes, all of them, are good medicine for the hole in our hearts. We need them all for balance, and we need to avoid overdosing on any of them, which is what happens when a man's psyche is not healed. Even what we call our needs may change if we practice them.

But a man must get on the court of life, get into the world, risk some projects. A few years ago, I was assisting in an event in which as a volunteer I was assigned to run microphones. What this entailed was running from the back of the room to get a mike to someone who'd raised his/her hand in my section. This could be ten to fifteen rows ahead, and the mike had a long cord. The point was to get it to the next speaker with promptness and grace. Sometimes the cord tangled up. Then someone coached me: Clinton, let the cord be a cord. I saw that that meant the cord was a cord—no more, no less. No more in that it didn't tangle or untangle itself by itself; no less because, if I handled it properly, it was a cord and served me. But the cord *didn't care* if I got it tangled, and I got aggravated with it—my wishes *per se* mattered not at all to it. The point is that the coaching I got was powerful because I was in the heat of handling the cord. I was on the court. The coaching wouldn't have been as powerful or meaningful if I had been sitting in my backyard thinking about running a microphone.

But now, I would like to pick up a topic we left behind, and only hinted at, back in Chapters 1 and 3—spirituality. In my view this is at the heart of the men's movement. How do I talk about spirituality? Someone said a *search* for God will not find him/her, that only *surrender* will. Maybe talking about it won't bring God (or higher power) closer either.

Spirituality is caring for one another and honoring the sanctity of life. It is also tying one's own shoes and feeling one's own feelings. It is an insight into what Paul called the unseen, which is eternal.[10] Spirit exists in implicate (unformed) energy and in silence. Spirit is vast and abundant. We are humble before its source. In spirit we are totally safe, whole, and free forever. Spirituality, though, is not the same as religion or religiosity. Central to religion is the institutionalized church that often generates dogma—which defines morality, controls people's lives, or makes war against nonbelievers. (Admittedly, churches also do some good things like care for others as a fellowship and offer rituals that promote harmony, unity, and ennoblement.)

Ritual is a central part of spirituality, and men who want to respond to the hole in their hearts will want to make use of it. Ritual is any standardized activity people do together that gives them a sense of connectivity with each other, with life, or with their bodies and the earth. It is usually carried out in a small space by only a few people at a time. Rituals invoke that which is sacred and powerful with the help of symbols and myths, which inspire virtue in individuals or challenge them for the good of the group, community, or society.[11]

I am even willing to take a radical position concerning ritual: without it there is no real men's group. Ritual is essential in men's groups, especially at the beginning and end of the meeting. It is one of the key ingredients that distinguishes a recovery men's group from a mere bull session. We may not always feel like doing ritual, and ritual may lose some of its significance when repeated for too long, but it is one of the forces that change us from a big "I" (arrogant ego) to a *group* member.

Unfortunately, ritual in small, private groups has gotten a bad name. People say that it characterizes dangerous, evil cults. That is not always true. In fact, when we omit ritual we insult "the other side," such things as our ancestry, the spirits, the earth, and the four directions. It is especially good medicine for me. I was raised to be a star. I want to do things *my* way. I want to stand out (and in some ways, that's good). When I am drumming, for example, with other men, I tell myself: *Get with the beat of the group, Clinton—there's something bigger here than you.* Ritual at the beginning brings some "contextual" power to the meeting, which can provide the space for transformative work to be done.

Good ritual can include some shadow stuff, which we mentioned earlier. Simply put, most of shadow work involves what we dislike in others, but are afraid to look at in ourselves—a shadow hangs over it. Egos (our defensive selves, which love to look good) and society's norms of conduct tend to push away that which we don't like or we don't want to face—for instance, death and our own tendencies toward rage, treachery, ugliness, and gore. We stress their opposites— *we're* cool, allegedly honest, or smart looking—but with a price. The shadows come out anyway. They cannot be suppressed. They manifest themselves as wars, crime, abuse, "nice" cheating and lying, or addictions. And usually we're sure that there are *other* people who are to blame for all these—if only we could have this nice little world of the few of us who are good all to ourselves.

Ritual, along with jokes, dreams, theatre productions, institutionalized aggression (for example, in competitive games), artistic acting out of our dark sides, and even bumper stickers ("I'm a dirty old man") gives vent to these suppressed aspects, which must be acknowledged as part of the *whole* of life.[12] Through ritual, with objects, masks, and motions, we can safely touch the dark sides, give them proper expression, and integrate them and their opposites into a new synthesis healthy for the psyche. Surprisingly, shadow work goes beyond the negatives that we shun, often in the name of self-righteousness; it includes our *noble* sides too. Society is often a conspiracy of muck and mediocrity. Misery loves company. Therefore, we're afraid to break these molds and express our remarkable goodness, effective actions, and magnanimity.

A couple of caveats may be in order. When I talk about the dark or shadow side of life, I am not necessarily talking about what some call evil. Evil has often been associated with the devil or generally with malevolent forces. A clear warrior/magician would probably stand up and rebuke (dismiss) such forces. Nor am I saying that doing shadow work precludes us from holding others accountable for atrocities and wrong-doing when those have been established.[13]

Perhaps a note now on the fierce and tender parts of men is in order. We return to Michael Meade's reference to fire and water.[14] The fire of life, pointed challenges especially, often awakens purpose in men—that's partly what's fierce, especially when it is well connected with a sense of the warrior that serves the king. The water, on the other hand, gives the tempering to men without which an exaggerated form of the warrior fire runs amok. The water also stands for grief and solitude, and only from them may tenderness arise.

A teaching I received about five years ago reminded me of the enormous power of water, a power I had not noticed before. Toward the close of a New Warrior training each man received a talisman. A talisman is a sack in which are wrapped some objects symbolic of one's good medicine. Among other things in the sack were some small stones from a brook. These had been worn smooth by the flow of water for many years. That's quite a lesson: It is the hard rocks that take shape by the slow force of the soft water.

EVALUATION

This chapter contains some ideas and terminology that may be troubling to some men (and women) in our society: wounds, archetypes, and rituals. This is understandable because wounds suggest being a victim or being identified with mental/emotional difficulties, which is very suspect in our culture because of the infamous cases of "crazy" people paraded before us in the mass media or in orally transmitted stories from generation to generation. It's easier to say, Oh yes, I'm fine, often meaning, I don't need any help, or don't have any wounds. Also, because we live in an era of scientific emphasis, archetypes and rituals may appear a little too far out—too superstitious. Additionally, some men may have had negative experiences with religion, which now turn them off to ritual as well. In men's work we might just change the language to ceremonials or dramatic enactments. Archetypes might be referred to as simply enduring ideas.

Finally, our urban way of life has separated us from natural (wild) animals and plants. Even worse, we may see them only as something in the way of progress or something to be taken dominion over. Then too, for some, there are negative connotations to terms like "wildman" and "warrior" in view of feminist critiques of patriarchy: if men are wild (it is thought), they are *bound* to be cruel or irresponsible; if men are freely sexual (it is thought), they are *bound* to be coercive.[15]

Some women, seeking to escape the strictures and sexism of traditional religions, have taken refuge in Goddess imagery. Sometimes their discussions include very harsh critiques of patriarchy and cruelties committed in the name of (male) gods. This is a subject beyond the scope of our present discussion. It deserves to be looked at carefully, but, in my opinion, men living their lives in integrity today should not be indicted by guilt by association even when the historical incidents are proven.[16] Also, men may choose to uphold *both* the father and mother God in their own lives.

NOTES AND REFERENCES

1. *New Age* (May, 1982), 30 passim 51.

2. Reading, Mass.: Addison-Wesley, 1990.

3. I use the word myth as a life-giving story for a people. Myths often express that which is in the code of life, especially how our lives connect with that which is transego or universal. They often contain hero stories of how mythological characters faced life's dilemmas and challenges, or they contain accounts of how ultimate questions are answered—for example, why bad things happen to good people, or how a society came about.

4. Also the sky and its cycles: night and day and the moon from partial to full.

5. As mentioned in Chapter 7, in a broad way, initiation involves a conscious process of marking a transition from one station or place in life to another. It opens a new beginning and is usually observed in ceremony in the company of others. With the help of teachers, initiation rites write their message deep into the initiate's psyche. The initiate moves from a comfortable space out into an unknown and uncomfortable space. This is the crucible. His survival allows him to return to life with a new and fuller identity and mission.

6. Robert Moore and Douglas Gillette, *King, Warrior, Magician, Lover* (New York: Harper-Collins, 1990).

7. Jung believed that archetypes are part of the design of the cosmos and that they are universal in that they are repeated in different times and places in spite of cultural differences. Our lives are played out through our conscious ego, according to this design. We can access the archetypes properly for good, or be run by them ruinously. The "inner" of the psyche gets played out as the "outer" of the archetypes. (See Moore and Gillette, Note 6.)

8. Sam Keen, *Fire in the Belly* (New York: Bantam, 1991), 29.

9. Keen, 41.

10. Holy Bible 2, Corinthians 4, 16–18.

11. See Wayne Liebman, *Tending the Fire: Ritual Men's Groups* (St. Paul, Minn.: Ally Press, 1991).

12. See T. J. Scheff, *Catharsis in Healing, Ritual and Drama* (Berkeley, Calif.: University of California Press, 1979).

13. See Robert Bly, *A Little Book on the Human Shadow* (San Francisco: Harper & Row, 1988) and Robert Johnson, *Owning Your Own Shadow* (San Francisco: Harper, 1991). Also, see an excellent feminist, postmodern

work on part of the shadow: Julia Kristeva (trans. by Leon S. Roudiez), *Strangers to Ourselves* (New York: Columbia University Press, 1991).

14. Michael Meade, *Men and the Water of Life* (San Francisco: Harper, 1993).

15. See John Rowan, *The Horned God: Feminism and Men As Wounding and Healing* (New York: Routledge, 1987).

16. See Riane Eisler, *The Chalice and the Blade* (San Francisco: Harper and Row, 1988). For a different view, see Aaron R. Kipnis, *Knights Without Armor* (Los Angeles, Jeremy P. Tarcher, 1991), Chapters 5–7.

Chapter 9

Intentional Men's Support Groups: An Opportunity to Take a Stand

Self-help groups, as an American creation, have been part of the landscape for thirty years or more. A perusal of directories will reveal an astonishing number of them, even in a small-sized city of thirty thousand people. A characteristic of these groups is that they have a clear focus, and they're dedicated to helping one another without the expertise or intervention of professionals. As such, they are profoundly equalitarian.

Men's groups are usually of that type. Groups of men can be created anywhere: in neighborhoods, through work, or in churches; however, they must be structured in certain ways to be productive.

My invitation to men to a workshop I offered in spring of '89 read:

I especially invite you if, in coming, you are willing to declare that your being there will make a difference. Gifts you can bring with you: Sorrow, anger (all forms), fear, resentment, and jealousy. We'll make silk purses from these.

Ten men came—even paid fifteen dollars each for the evening of work. We had a great time. I learned a lot from them.

Despite the recent awareness and publicity, some men still find the idea of men's groups as odd or even silly—silly until one jumps in and does it. In considering one, a man is taking a risk: He will be exposing a different side of himself. And just in *starting* this new commitment in his life, he may rock the boat with those who are left behind. The result, however, is usually highly beneficial to all—those in the group and those not. I hardly ever want to go to my men's group meeting. Then, after it is over, I'm so glad I did. The intention is not, or should not be, to keep secrets discussed in the men's group away from someone like a spouse or a significant other, but rather to have a safe place, and often useful, comforting feedback, to explore issues, which later, one might be better able to open with one's loved ones.

One of my objectives in men's work, as well as empowering work with all people, is to assist in opening up possibilities in men's lives—to bring something into the present that they hadn't seen before. Let me illustrate. In the fall of 1987 when I went to Moscow to run in the International Peace Marathon, I took a Polaroid camera; I had taken a crash eight-week course in Russian before we left. After I ran my 10-K, I retrieved my camera from a friend on the sidelines who had been holding it for me. I began to take some pictures. I saw a group of about twenty Soviet soldiers, standing in rank and file by the large water cans. They all looked quite stern and serious.

I caught the eye of one on the end and in my broken Russian asked him if he'd take my picture. He stepped out and did so, noticing that it was an "instant" camera. Quickly, I asked him if I could take *his* picture. Suddenly the stern countenance broke, and possibility seemed to light up for him like a light bulb. As I was about to snap his picture, something very unexpected happened. Possibility spread. All nineteen of his comrades broke rank and piled in behind him to be in the picture too. Their faces also changed just as had the first soldier's. I began to snap away, and, after each time, one soldier would jump up and grab the picture, which was about to develop before his very eyes.

We were "having a riot," as they say, and it went one step further. As our American women world runners came across the finish line, the soldiers began to pull them into their group too, and I took more pictures of all of them. I took at least twenty photographs there and gave them all away to the soldiers. I figure it was one of the best investments I've ever made.

I see that when possibility opens for people, a paradigm usually shifts too. In this case, for the first soldier, it was the view that he had an opportunity not present the minute before. He could be someone new. He didn't have to *think* about it much. It's as if the possibility called *him* forth. This can occur on a small scale (as here) or on a large scale with thousands of people. Men's work that does this is likely to be very successful.

It is not as hard to start a group as one might think—you can invite men by word of mouth, person to person, or by an announcement/invitation in front of a group or even one published in a newspaper. It is important, however, to be upfront and as clear about purpose as possible. You may want to interview prospective members. Some may not be suitable because they have needs or problems that are better handled in therapy. You must ask men to make a commitment, maybe at first to only three or four meetings before they decide whether to stay in the group or not. Structure can be decided upon in the first few meetings. Optimum size may be around seven to twelve and usually the wider the range of ages the better. Diversity of men in terms of points of view, sexual orientation, religion, wealth, or color is fine also. Don't wait until you have all the expert advice needed for either setting up a men's gathering or participating in an ongoing group. Not knowing how or what to do (and discussing that with others) is nurturing—so is making mistakes. It is not unusual for men previously unknown to each other to initially feel hostile toward each other in the group and not say anything about it.[1]

I prefer a number of guidelines for on-going support groups:

1. A secure physical space (room) is needed, which maximizes privacy and minimizes any interruptions. This is both a sanctuary and the work area. An altar or centerpiece is good, too.

2. After some trial meetings, it's okay if a man not aligned with the group's intention chooses to not be in the group. Bless him on his way. For those who stay, request that they make an explicit declaration to that effect in front of the group.

3. If a man misses two or more consecutive meetings, he ought to clear himself when reentering the group being as honest with himself and the group as possible.

4. If a man is going to miss or be tardy at a group meeting, he ought to call another member of the group if possible to let him know.

5. If a man uses drugs or alcohol within six hours prior to a meeting, he agrees to let the group know.
6. The meaning of confidentiality should be discussed in the group, and then a standing request be made to all that, if it is violated, it may be cleaned up by apologies and the creation of new rules or understandings if necessary.
7. Men in the group are urged to speak directly to each other and to use "I" statements, the language of self-responsibility, as much as possible.
8. Anyone may pass at anytime, that is, decline to participate in a reading or a hug.
9. Any decision to leave the group, after making the initial commitment to stay, should be processed and acknowledged in the group.[2]

These guidelines look like I am suggesting a tight ship. That's true. There's at least one good reason for that. Good men's work doesn't happen by accident. It must be intentional, and structuring a group in these ways helps. At the same time, I say pick and choose or modify (experiment with) any of these guidelines or ones that follow.

Groups are free to choose their own format and agenda (for example, in regard to taking turns in leading the meeting), but in all cases it should be made clear that the meetings are not simply bull sessions. All men should be warmly welcomed and generously acknowledged. I see acknowledgment as somewhat different from what we usually call compliments. When acknowledging another I am speaking for the way another person shows up for me. It is not syrupy praise nor necessarily the long list of his achievements. Rather, it speaks to the integrity, honesty, and joy, he inspires in me. Another version says: Catch people doing good and let them know.

In men's groups we do both inner (for example, feelings) and outer (mission) work. Call this initiation work if you like.

I see groups as dividing into two parts or phases: First, men may want to get together to mainly share. The meeting could go something like this: It begins and closes at a prearranged time. A brief (maybe two or three minutes, maximum) check-in opportunity is afforded to each man when he states as clearly and as succinctly as possible where he is in terms of his feelings and concerns. (Anything more that he may want to share or work on, whether about sex, money, work, family, or health, he holds until all men have done their check-ins). When a man is checking in, it's important that the others just listen attentively. This is one of the ways men bless other men. If a man is going further after all the check-ins, the others may ask him what he would like or what he needs from the group—resources, advice, just listening, telephone calls during the week, whatever would be most helpful.

Second, a group can go much deeper. Several different experiences or experiments are suggested: 1) It can engage in collective rituals such as drumming, praying (to any source of life), singing, or dancing, done in unison or together, and share stories of the type Bly or Meade use to make the archetypes or heroes more real. 2) It can perform structured exercise on trust, listening, feeling, communication, self-acceptance, or self-expression.[3] This can include visualizations, coloring pictures, speaking affirmations, rolling in the mud, making "emotion faces" or noises while looking in a mirror, writing a letter to one's father, sharing experiences regarding incidents where we felt ashamed or humiliated, catching each other in a backwards free-fall, or making masks. 3) It can perform some (re)enactments. Usually these take the form of one group member going back in his past, and, with another man acting as the father, mother, or whoever, the first addresses the second with all the feeling he can muster. Role-reversals can also be used. The purpose is usually catharsis, insight, and completion. 4) Men can develop a mission (vision) statement for their lives and, with staff in hand, read it with passion in front of the group.

They might also take on fixing some long-held complaint, the completion of which is to be measured by particular results. I call this a project. A project is an especially powerful exercise, since it may stretch a man, break him out of his business as usual daily (comfort zone) life, provide openings for self-generated declarations, and anchor him in a mode of efficacy (which is especially good balance for flying men/boys).

I recommend the following structure for a project: (1) Choose a complaint that is significant and doable (fixable) in six to ten weeks. Who is to blame for it is not relevant, but the accomplishment of the project must make a real difference in one's life. Alterations in diet, exercise, saving money, work, family, environment, service to others, or letter-writing to politicians are all prospects. (2) Declare your intention to the group and to at least five people outside the group: For example, I'm going to lose fifteen pounds by (*a given date*). (3) Visualize a wide range of benefits that might accrue to you and/or others as a result of your fixing this complaint. (This is powerful as a pull since we so often rely in this culture on the push of punishment for *not* doing it.) (4) Enlist others to assist you if that's appropriate. (5) Request the support of two committed listeners who are accessible, who know your project and its substeps in detail, and to whom you promise to check in daily or semidaily regarding your progress. They also promise to hear your breakdowns, clear you when they occur, and hear your declaration to return on course after you've learned what there is to learn from the breakdowns. (6) Do the project and outrageously celebrate its completion even if your results fall short. (7) Now one might even see the possibility of making a larger stand out of this (more than weight loss). For example, one may decide to take a stand for the physical well being of other people, which could involve further projects requiring more people. (8) The men's group as a whole may also choose to take on a service project for others outside the group: befriend, serve, or hold in their heart some old men or some youths at risk of delinquency, or work for some women's rights goals. In summary, it must be said that a project is not something to make a man's life busier—most of them are too busy already—but rather to empower him in the area of priorities and steady focus.

Sometimes in the men's group to which I belonged we engaged in more confrontation and laying of new track in our lives as commitment born of desire or vision, or we provided more openings for the expression of sorrow, fear, and anger. When a big project was inaugurated out of an important stand, our familiar vicissitudes diminished in import. This is what happened when I took on the going-to-Moscow-to-run project out of my stand for the end of hunger on the planet. "Here am I, send me." In all, however, it was important to create a safe environment, bless and acknowledge each other, give each an opportunity to check in and maybe take a stand, get us out of our heads (defensive intellectualizations) and into our guts. If men choose to go deeper, they will when they're ready or when it seems appropriate.

If they don't, that's okay too. Some men will need and ask for a lot of comfort from the group. That's fine. Others will want to move ahead to some challenging initiations and projects. That's fine also.

If you're a normal human being, you probably know the game called "wanting what you can't have." It's probably endemic to the human condition but exacerbated in our society due to our acquisitiveness. I play it many times a day, and I have seen it come up in men's groups often. The game may be quite legitimate as when we imagine outcomes that would enhance our lives but that seem difficult to obtain. Some facets of the game may be worth examining: What do we really want? Is it o.k. to want what we want? Are we sure we can't have it? Are we first grateful for what we do have?

Some versions of the game, though, may be self-betraying as when it seems others around us are doing so much better than we are. In this case, what we want is to be more like them or to have what they have. In short, life may look like it is always better over there. And sometimes it might be, but we may also be seeing the *protected* self of others, their strategic interaction (best foot forward), and we compare this to our raw self, our keen sense of our own inadequacies. This is especially true in our society where people tend to smile a lot and look carefree and successful. What may be even more eye opening is to find that others may be secretly perceiving *you* as so much better or happier than they.

Feelings are likely to be a big part of men's groups, and it is appropriate to make a few observations about them. There are thoughts, and there are feelings. They are not the same, although they can affect one another. I see that our everyday language in the matter is sloppy. For example, when a man says, "I feel that Russia will invade the Ukraine," he's really not overtly speaking of feeling at all, but rather (apparently) of something he *thinks* or expects. Maybe he means: "I'm *afraid* Russia will invade the Ukraine."

There are only four basic feelings or emotions: sad, glad, mad, and scared. There are, of course, combinations of these, and there are some, such as embarrassment, that have many cognitive components blended in (for example, I *thought* I looked silly standing there with my zipper open and I *felt* mad at myself for not remembering to close it before I got up in front of the class. I was so embarrassed.).

Feelings or emotions are universal among all human kind, but what triggers them is our cognitive interpretation of events given to us in our culture. It is, therefore, appropriate to be angry when such and such happens here, but perhaps not so in another society or group.

In the year or two before my divorce I began to discover that there were ways of dealing with my feelings that served my well being (and the safety and dignity of others), and ways that did not. In short, what worked was to name the feeling, to allow myself to feel it, experience it, and to talk about it with a few other people. For many years, talking about feelings was always easier with women. I'm still grateful for that. Now, since being in men's groups, I prefer men—there's a different reality when sharing with another man, especially one who is on a recovery journey.

Back to the basic emotions. Sadness has much of its source in loss; anger's source may be in being hurt, cheated, violated, or it may be a response to loss also; fear's source may be in the unknown or in the anticipation of something painful or undesirable; joy's source lies in accomplishment or the restoration of well being.

Anger is one emotion that frequently comes up with men, and I'd like to discuss some of its variants. In growing up I had seen very few instances of clear anger—usually it was expressed in pouting, blaming, or violence. Often it was delayed and repressed so that the next irritating event triggered disproportionate anger or (out of control) rage.

A surprise was in store for me in a men's workshop when I was encouraged to go to the bottom of my rage in a safe space.[4] It's probably not true for everyone, but in some ways I'm a show-me guy, or one who says, I'm going to try it. I went totally all-out on rage, and it was more than a mock-up—it was real. To my surprise I saw that fearing the rage was in many ways worse than "being there." When I was finished I had a sense of relief, like going through a haunted house and coming out intact: I've been there; now I know I can survive. It was my own rage which I feared during much of my life.

1. Sometimes anger was triggered when another criticized me, especially when I knew it was true. I was taught to protect my inadequacies, even my wrongs.
2. Sometimes I used anger in an attempt to control another. They might be scared of my anger if they didn't do what I wanted.
3. Sometimes anger was triggered when (I thought) someone threatened to take something I needed (like my wife).
4. Often anger overlaid fear—fear of being abandoned, fear of being hurt (again), fear of losing—or frustration (I cannot get it all done or It's too hard for me.)
5. Sometimes anger, especially long-term anger, was a sign that I was putting up with something that I should not be.

Whatever the type of anger (or resentment), it was good to take responsibility for it and talk about it in a safe place. I began to practice speaking it with passion: "I'm angry!"—and, then, *let it go.* Also anger-energy can be quite useful in moving us forward in our life, to taking on the question, What am I going to *do* about it? It should not be denied.

Over the years, while participating in support groups, I have noticed, in my life and through people's sharing, some patterns regarding emotions. Some learn early on a distinction they call "expressing" versus "showing" one's emotions. Showing can involve communication such as I'll get back at him/her (for example, tell him/her off)—he/she will *know* how I feel. Or sometimes showing feelings involves quiet (calculated) withdrawal so the other will know (suspect) I'm hurt (martyred?), or maybe it involves the bargaining that, If he/she knows I'm hurt, they won't *make* me disappointed anymore. There is, of course, a fine line on the one hand between letting them know how I feel, and that I expect (demand) a change in their behavior.

On the other hand, expressing my feelings may mean I learn to keep my mouth shut at times—that I call another (neutral) person to whom I can vent my feelings safely, and that I honor my feelings as a part of my humanity.

In my own life, for the most part, I had suppressed the expression of feelings until into my forties when my crises seemed to trigger them.

I observed several patterns: 1) When emotions came pouring in early on, I was like a yo-yo—they took me up and down. I seemed to have little power in the matter; 2) I also became a lightning rod —I'd pick up the feeling from others, and they'd go right through me and move me up or down; and 3) I finally got a healthy point of vantage (sometimes) on my feelings—like almost seeing them (my feelings) as a "witness"—something I *had* and experienced, but which didn't necessarily run me in terms of what I thought I was compelled to do as a result of the feelings, especially when what I might do would get me into trouble.

Emotion work is a good place to start in men's groups, but in my opinion, we shouldn't get stuck there; it is not the end. Projects are. More precisely it's what projects can teach us as we get on the court. Moreover, if I opine that I cannot start a project until I've handled my feelings, the wait may be a very long one.

I turn now to another gathering for comparison—Alcoholics Anonymous—which brings together men and women, black and white, old and young, from all walks of life. I want to start with the serenity prayer:

> God grant me the serenity
> to accept the things I cannot change,
> courage to change the things I can,
> and wisdom to know the difference.

When a man (or a woman) drinks alcohol to kill the pain or sorrow in his life, and does so compulsively, his life is likely to go from bad to worse even though, at first, alcohol seems to do *wonderful* things for him.

The scene is a community room in a local hospital and sixty to eighty men, and a few women, have gathered on Saturday night for an open Alcoholics Anonymous meeting where shades of Bill W., its founder in 1935, still linger.[5] I've gone to these meetings for four years; I love the hugs we give each other.[6] You don't have to have a college degree or a high-status job to participate. It looks like rag-tag assembly—most men are dressed in plain shirt and trousers, some in motorcycle clothes, and a few a little fancier. Whatever the appearance, these people are here because they know their life depends on it. There is urgency, ritual, deep sharing, and clear acknowledgment. Recently, the speaker sharing his story opened by saying: "It's fabulous to be living a sober life."

These men and women have been through the dark night of the soul. At some point or points they looked into their crisis, took full responsibility, made amends to those they had harmed, and surrendered to the "power greater than ourselves," which is mentioned in the second step of the program. Now, through the dogged support of others and a sponsor, they have a choice: bitterness or gratitude. Most choose gratitude, and you have to hear it directly, and in person, to appreciate it. They're *living* it one day at a time. It is very moving. These are indeed twice-born men, and they range in age from seventeen to ninety-one. Their stories vary, but all speak of a turn-around, a healing, a need to stay clean, and a need to "give it away" by now being of service to others. They've, many of them, gone beyond sobriety to actual joy in their lives.

When a man "works a program," at the core of which are the twelve steps, he is addressing problems of living, not just problems of alcohol; and he is taking on something both vertically and horizontally bigger than himself, at least bigger than the way he usually has regarded himself. That is, vertically, he begins an examination inward, which offers an opportunity for a connection to higher power that includes his own honesty, surrender, and conversation with other men. Horizontally, it's larger because working a program takes a whole lifetime or more—there's always further to go.

But I'm sitting there in these meetings, perplexed: Why haven't more of the eighteen to twenty-three-year-old men in my classes awakened? They still seem to drift or stay in the fog. A few answers seem appropriate: they're still dependent on their parents—it's extended adolescence time in our society since urbanism made children and their labor obsolete. They haven't been out on their own. Another possibility is that they linger in the opiate of the dating-rating complex in our society, and in the culture of cross-gender romance. They are preparing for careers and may actually be doing quite well. They haven't been alone long enough to face the demons within; they haven't gone through a crisis that shakes one to the very core of survival.

In this regard, oddly enough, a few of the recovering men make reference to the blessing in disguise of their alcoholism, as if it were a strange gift. Going through it, seeing that "My life doesn't work," "I'm in *big* trouble," "I alone am responsible and there is help, and I have to want it with all my heart and *ask* for it," these recognitions seem to be the gift. Then comes a new opening for redesigning one's life—even giving up the debilities of destructive gender roles and false pride (arrogance). Eric Hoffer, a very remarkable man, was once asked in an interview by Bill Moyers why it was that so many men enjoyed his company, especially the many longshoremen with whom he chatted at the docks. Hoffer's answer was something like, I make sure I learn something from each—that I let each teach me something. True humility. This is what I hear from many of the recovering alcoholics.

Spirituality may be the other answer why many of my students have not heard the wake-up call. Men do not live by bread alone. A man must walk his valley of the shadow alone; he must sit in the woods shivering and afraid of the howl of the wolves around him as in male initiations among the Sioux, but he must know eventually that he really is never alone. He must find out for himself.

Make no mistake about it. I offer neither AA, male initiation, nor men's groups/networks as a one-shot panacea. The road is long, the work messy. Be apprised. Men in men's groups might break down and cry deeply, painfully. The temptation will be to rescue them, to ease their pain. Let them be, unless they're asking for assistance that is appropriate. Often, gold lies at the end of the pain for them if they go through it honestly. Sometimes, too, men will get into deep conflict with other men in the group. This is normal, too, and can be growthful. Let them address each other within the boundaries of rules for fair fighting (that is, without physical violence). Sometimes a man talks as a stuck record, speaking the same problem over and over, week after week. It may be time to confront him: What's his gut feelings in the matter? What is the truth for *him* in this matter? we ask him. Is he willing to do anything about it, or is he just getting the payoff of complaining or feeling bad? All this work will be useful on the outside too—with children, spouse, or employer. What I am doing is calling us into the possibility of a new way of life—out of the swirls of entanglement, down into the dark, out of shame and useless anger, into missions and projects.

Now we are approaching the end of our journey for this book. What, might we ask, is commonly lacking when a men's group goes flat? Let us start with a very short story, which includes a man, a fire, and some wood. The man stands cold before the fire and demands: "Fire, fire, give me heat." But, the fire answers "First, you must give me more wood." So it was in my life—I was standing by a dying fire demanding more heat (from life or from others). One of the first places to look when men's groups go flat is to the question, What is each of us putting into them (the wood)? Of course, the best place to start is with myself—*What am I contributing?*

Secondly, look for "withholds." These are disagreements, disappointments, or broken agreements among the men in the group (or in their separate lives with others outside the group), which are not being verbalized, but should be. Thirdly, look for a lack of missions undertaken and declared in the group that are going to be carried out outside the group and which will make a difference in the quality of peoples' lives. Fourthly, look for a slow-down in acknowledgments— genuine words of inspiration spoken one man to another in the group and to others outside the group.

Fifthly, use some closer listening in the group and be ready for surprises. For example, recently, I came to our group meeting and got comfortable (in a big bean-bag chair)—too comfortable. While we were each, in turn, doing our check-ins a man (whom I did not expect) dropped a hint regarding another issue in his life. I missed it, but another man in the group caught it and, after all the check-ins were completed, invited the man to bring the issue before the group. To my surprise, he did. (I thought he was shy.) In fact, he spoke it so honestly that it quickly ignited the group—others had the same or a very similar issue. His risk-taking made the whole evening very worthwhile to me.

Finally, in some cases, it may be time to disband the group as a group and give it a decent burial.

In closing I'd like to underscore the importance of play. Play is an activity that has only a recreational purpose. It's hard to play in this culture. Some of my students seem to think that play is when you overindulge in something, break the routine, pay for it by discomfort or harm to oneself or others later. They prove that they are *free* to do as they like. That's not what I mean by play. What's closer to it is what I see my little terrier dog, Mouse, do when we go out to an open field near my house for a walk or run.

When we get to the field, I unleash her and I notice she totally revels in the sights, sounds, and smells around her. She needs little reason to be fully vibrant. Moreover, when she darts here or there, she never proceeds in a straight line like I do. Doesn't she know the laws of geometry—that the shortest distance between two points is a *straight* line? That's how you conserve effort, isn't it? Yes, but play is not primarily about that. Play is vital for people. It must be connected to men's groups or they die. Take some time to do it.

EVALUATION

The question can be raised as to how to evaluate the men's movement? That seems to be fair. As a point of comparison, we might ask how people have evaluated the women's movement. In this regard a number of facets came to mind: 1) Was there an impact on our thinking regarding the rights and dignity of women? Did this show up in national opinion polls? 2) Was there some successful legislation passed at various political levels? 3) Was there any change in individual women's ways of going about their everyday life in, for example, habits of child-rearing, aspirations in employment, or criticality of religion? 4) Did women who joined consciousness-raising groups intensify their re-orientation to women's issues? Did these processes have a long-term effect?

The men's movement is quite new. A few evaluation studies are being done, and their results are not yet available.[7] Some of them take a before—and after design. That is, men who've been active in ongoing men's groups recall how it was for them before getting involved and how it is now in terms of benefits to themselves and others. Perhaps some control groups will be used too, that is, other men of similar social background who have not gotten involved can be compared to those who are involved in terms of changes in thinking regarding men's inherent dignity, as well as changes in fathering, outreach to other men (for example, men in prisons and gangs), and partnership with women.

We would expect the area of evaluation to be slippery: how much is a movement worth if it affects for the good the lives of even a few men? When is a critical mass reached in terms of numbers of men involved such that a major shift in consciousness and practice is reached? These are questions to keep before us.

NOTES AND REFERENCES

1. Many readers, perhaps mainly women, might have been asking me, What about male violence? Admittedly, I have not fully addressed that issue. Back in Chapter 2 we mentioned the war that men may engage in against men from another (neighboring) society, when members of the first society perceive the second to be encroaching or threatening to steal/plunder from them. That is probably legitimate, especially given the limited modes of conflict resolution available.

What women more often seem to be asking is, What about men and their violence today? Let me tell a little story. I was recently a beginning student in a martial arts class (Tai Chi). The instructor asked for a volunteer in regard to his demonstration of the defensive power of Tai Chi. Of course, I volunteered (I almost always do). He assured me, in front of the class, that I would not be harmed. When we went into stance, he apparently thought I was a veteran (just by the way I held my arms). Suddenly, like being hit by a cyclone to the fiftieth power, I found myself on the floor fifteen feet behind where I had been standing. My elbow and knee were hurting, but I got up and, to his inquiry, said I was o.k. Later that evening, at home, I called him and confronted him with what had happened to me, and, he, later, apologized in front of the whole class.

I tell the story for several reasons. As a man I really thought it was necessary to hide (deny) my pain and my perception of trust broken by him. I also want to say that if we continue to ignore the causes of men's contemporary violence, at home or on the street, and "treat" their violence by throwing them in (more violent) prisons, we will surely be faced by *more* of those questions the women ask: What about male violence?

2. If the men's group has become quite cohesive, someone leaving may be perceived as a threat to the group, and there may be some blame-sending that occurs either from the group to the person leaving or *vice versa*. I recommend that both the group and the person leaving examine whether there are some deficits that can be corrected, but not to get into lengthy explanations of blame or defensiveness beyond that. In the Al-Anon groups to which I belong, people come and go quite freely. When someone is missing for awhile s/he may get a call from someone in the group saying, Are you o.k? I miss you, but when "principles come before personalities" (part of the twelve-step commitment), gossip or "wrong-making" is unnecessary when someone drops out.

3. There are many exercises available. Two I especially like: 1) The men stand in a circle and one by one a man looks into the eyes of the man on his left and tells him: "I am (his name). I am your brother. I stand beside you." That's all, and then we go on to the next man who does the same. If done with clear respect, this is a very moving/touching process. 2) Each man gets a turn at saying, "If I were a bad boy/man, I'd say/do_____ ." This can be very hilarious and/or serious and healing if men really put themselves into it and, also, feel what they feel with each statement and share the feeling with the group. See Bill Kauth, *A Circle of Men: The Original Men's Support Group Manual* (New York: St. Martin's Press, 1992) and Merle Fossum, *Catching Fire: Men Coming Alive in Recovery* (San Francisco: Harper and Row, 1989).

4. It must be emphasized that some processes, such as this one, must not be done without the guidance of trained personnel.

5. *Alcoholics Anonymous* (New York: Alcoholics Anonymous World Services, Inc., 1976).

6. There is another important reason why I, and perhaps others, go also. Now that I am no longer surrounded by a biological family, going to the Al-Anon or Alcoholics Anonymous fellowships help keep me in touch with the mundane, but highly important, affairs of everyday life from the standpoint of the individual and his larger life space—affairs of marriages, divorces, work, children, celebrations, money, death, or relatives.

7. Some are now being received at The Changing Men Collections at The Michigan State University's Libraries, East Lansing, Michigan 48824–1048.

Selected Bibliography

August, Eugene R. 1994. *The New Men's Studies: A Selected and Annotated Bibliography*. Englewood, CO: Libraries Unlimited, Incorporated.

Blankenhorn, David. 1995. *Fatherless America*. New York: Basic Books.

Bly, Robert. 1990. *Iron John*. Reading, MA: Addison-Wesley.

Brod, Harry, and Kaufman, Michael. 1994. *Theorizing Masculinities*. Thousand Oaks, CA: Sage Publications, Incorporated.

Connell, R. W. 1995. *Masculinities*. Berkeley, CA: University of California Press.

Corneau, Guy. 1991. *Absent Fathers, Lost Sons*. Boston, MA: Shambala.

Doyle, James A. 1995. *The Male Experience*. Madison, WI: Wm. C. Brown.

Farrell, Warren. 1993. *The Myth of Male Power*. New York: Simon & Schuster.

Farrell, Warren. 1986. *Why Men Are The Way They Are*. New York: McGraw-Hill.

Fossum, Merle. 1989. *Catching Fire: Men Coming Alive in Recovery*. New York: Harper.

Franklin, Clyde W. II. 1994. *The Changing Definition of Masculinity*. New York: Plenum Press.

Franklin, Clyde W. II. 1988. *Men & Society*. Chicago, IL: Nelson-Hall, Incorporated.

Gerson, Kathleen. 1993. *No Man's Land: Men's Changing Commitments to Family and Work*. New York: Basic Books.

Goldberg, Herb. 1976. *The Hazards of Being Male*. New York: New American Library.

Griswold, Robert L. 1993. *Fatherhood in America*. New York: Basic Books.

Harding, Christopher. ed. 1992. *Wingspan: Inside The Men's Movement*. New York: St. Martin's Press.

Kauth, Bill. 1992. *A Circle of Men: The Original Manual for Men's Support Groups*. New York: St. Martin's Press.

Keen, Sam. 1991. *Fire in the Belly*. New York: Bantam Books.

Keillor, Garrison. 1993. *The Book of Guys*. New York: Viking Penguin.

Kilmartin, Christopher T. 1994. *The Masculine Self*. New York: McMillan.

Kimbrell, Andrew. 1995. *The Masculine Mystique: The Politics of Masculinity*. New York: Ballantine.

Kimmel, Michael S. 1996. *Manhood in America: A Cultural History*. New York: Free Press.

Kimmel, Michael S. ed. 1995. *The Politics of Manhood*. Philadelphia: Temple University Press.

Kimmel, Michael S. and Messner, Michael A. eds. 1995. *Men's Lives*. 3d ed. Boston, MA: Allyn and Bacon.

Kipnis, Aaron R. 1991. *Knights Without Armor*. Los Angeles: Jeremy P. Tarcher.

Lee, John. 1991. *At My Father's Wedding*. New York: Bantam.

Levant, Ronald F. and Pollack, William S. eds. 1995. *A New Psychology of Men*. New York: Basic Books.

Meade, Michael. 1993. *Men and the Water of Life*. New York: Harper Collins.

Moore, Robert and Gillette, Douglas. 1990. *King Warrior Magician Lover: Rediscovering the Archetypes of the Mature Masculine*. New York: Harper.

Osherson, Samuel. 1986. *Finding Our Fathers*. New York: The Free Press.

Osherson, Samuel. 1992. *Wrestling With Love*. New York: Fawcett Columbine.

Pleck, Joseph H. 1981. *The Myth of Masculinity*. Cambridge, MA: The MIT Press.

Rubin, Lillian. 1983. *Intimate Strangers*. New York: Harper & Row.

Ruth, Sheila. 1995. *Issues in Feminism*. 3d ed. Mountain View, CA: Mayfield Publishing Company.

Schenk, Roy U. and Everingham, John. eds. 1995. *Men Healing Shame*. New York: Springer.

Thompson, Keith. ed. 1991. *To Be A Man*. Los Angeles: Jeremy P. Tarcher.

Warshak, Richard A. 1992. *The Custody Revolution*. New York: Poseidon Press.

Index

Warrior, 29
"What Men Really Want"
   (Bly), 99
Wingspan, 14
"Withholds," 123
Women, Men, and Society, 7
Women's studies, 3–5
Work, 85–88; husbands and

wives compared 81;
middle class, 86; mis-
sion of, 87–88; reasons
for, 85; support laws,
86; working class, 87
Wound, 100–101

Yielding, 69

About the Author

CLINTON J. JESSER is Professor of Sociology at Northern Illinois University where he was co-founder of the Women's Studies Program and co-founder of DeKalb's Women's shelter. Dr. Jesser has been a teacher/researcher and writer in the area of sex and gender for 25 years. For the last eight years, he has participated in men's work, especially the New Warrior Network and 12-step groups.

Vicissitudes.